When the Heavens Go Quiet

A Book About Belief, Doubt, and Evidence
by Noah Baer

When the Heavens Go Quiet
First Edition, July 2025
Published by Late Sky Press
Printed in the United States of America
ISBN: 979-8-9992328-0-9

Cover design by Late Sky Press
Interior design by Noah Baer

This is a work of nonfiction. While every effort has been made to ensure accuracy, the author makes no representations or warranties about the completeness or applicability of the content. The views and opinions expressed are solely those of the author.

For permissions, inquiries, or more information:
Late Sky Press

"I would rather have questions that can't be answered than answers that can't be questioned."
— *Richard Feynman*

"Comfort is not a measure of truth. Truth is not gentle; it does not cradle the heart. It is dense, indifferent, and solitary. It carries no promises, only clarity."

— *Noah Baer*

1

The Cognitive Roots of Faith and Science

The search for answers to the unknown has long been a defining conflict within consciousness (a natural expression of curiosity). It is an experience inherent to the human condition. Where humanity chooses to direct that curiosity, and how it constructs personal truths in the face of uncertainty, gives rise to an enduring sense of 'something more.' This ongoing tension between the intuitive comfort of belief and the rigorous discomfort of scientific inquiry has shaped the evolution of human understanding. Though both stem from the same drive to explain the unknown, they diverge in method, purpose, and consequence. This chapter explores the psychological, evolutionary, and philosophical roots of belief and scientific inquiry.

Before tides were understood as the result of gravitational interactions between Earth, the moon, and the sun, they were attributed to Poseidon, the God of the sea. For people in the 11th century BC, this seemed like a rational explanation.

God: a superhuman being or spirit worshiped as having power over nature or human fortunes. Looking at Poseidon in the eyes of an 11th-century BC Greek, it makes sense that a God caused the ocean tides. If one were to criticize or question the validity of the gods or deity that their community accepted, they would be exiled or even executed. Socrates, an Athenian philosopher and considered by most to be the founder of Western philosophy, was executed for teaching philosophical questioning to his students. These critical thinking abilities that Socrates sought to pass down to future generations were countered by the sophists and their cultural contributions. The same contributions that create halts in scientific progression due to intimidation and a fear of thinking beyond the assigned God they were given at a young, impressionable age.

Religion once filled the roles that science fills today. Yet, there are still modern equivalents to the ancient believers of Poseidon (those who are satisfied with spiritual or religious explanations and see no need to question further). One can understand why the species attributed elusive notions to the Gods before the advent of the Newtonian way of thinking. This stems from the lack of conclusive analytical data or a standardized scientific method before Isaac Newton. Newton is considered a safe starting point for science because he was one of the first to believe that scientific theory should be coupled with rigorous experimentation. This principle ultimately led to the development of modern science. This is also a practical starting point, sidestepping debates over whether science began earlier with figures like Aristotle, often referred to as the first scientist, despite the term 'science' emerging centuries later. For the sake of the chapter, Modern science will begin with Isaac Newton.

In modern science, whenever a discovery is published, particularly one that alters society, every scientist conducts the same tests and applies the same math to validate or disprove the results. In Karl

Popper's book, *The Logic of Scientific Discovery*, he states that a theory or hypothesis is considered falsifiable if it can be proven wrong through empirical testing or observation. This makes perfect sense and is even quite simple. This is the same logic that deemed Poseidon a delusion. One can only do such deeming after the belief has been proven falsifiable through empirical testing or observation. If the publisher ignores these contradictions, that is where delusion starts to arise, or the sense of more from a content standpoint. If the species can use this logic of soundness to discredit old notions of religion and current scientific publications, then why are there still those satisfied with spiritual or religious explanations and see no need to question further? Defining religious explanations as accepting the unknown without verifiable evidence, but rather firsthand experience or faith.

This human tendency to accept beliefs without evidence is what baffles scientists. Scientists question: If humanity has the tools to examine and test the unknown, why do some stop at unverified explanations? From a materialistic perspective, it comes down to the way a specific person's neurochemistry has evolved. If their developmental path resulted in it being more advantageous or even regular for them to feel comfortable in not questioning the unknown, then that would explain why some still accept the unknown without evidence. The question that arises now is why the brain would evolve to favor belief without proof. The agency detection is a psychological trait shaped by evolution that leads to the interpretation of events as being caused by intentional actions. For example, a person walks alone through the woods at night. Suddenly, a branch snaps somewhere behind them. Their heart races, and they immediately think, "Someone's following me." Even though it could easily be the wind, a falling branch, or an animal, their brain instinctively jumps to the idea of an agent— a person or creature with intent. That reaction is their built-in agent detection system doing its job. This is thanks to a chemical called dopamine. Dopamine is mainly responsible for pleasure and satisfaction, but also heightens attention and reinforces pattern recognition. For instance, when one's brain detects something unexpected, such as a branch snapping, dopamine helps process the pattern. This detection and procedure often lead the mind to think that an agent is at work. From an evolutionary standpoint, this explains why a false positive is safer than a false negative.

The fact that human brains are primed for agent detection means that they should perceive intentional agents even when they are not present. That's not all, the brain will also assign purpose to random events and seek meaning in chaos. This all sounds familiar, almost like the foundation of theism itself—The brain's attempt to find divine intention in randomness and sacred order in the chaos of existence.

Over time, these individual instincts—detecting agency, assigning purpose, and seeking meaning did not remain isolated thoughts. They were reinforced through shared narratives, stories, and rituals. What began as a survival-driven mental reflex evolved into mythology and eventually became organized religions. These systems codified the belief in unseen agents, offering not only explanations for natural events but also social cohesion, moral structure, and existential comfort. Religious practices such as prayer, meditation, and communal worship often trigger the brain's reward systems. Dopamine and serotonin levels rise, creating feelings of peace, connection, and euphoria. In this way, religion becomes neurologically self-reinforcing. It not only explains the world, but it feels good to believe.

Humans don't only believe for pleasure but also to manage fear and loss. This fear could stem from thanatophobia, which in summary is the fear of death. Being aware of one's mortality is a unique characteristic of the human species. Humans are perhaps the only species capable of comprehending their mortality. In response to this awareness, religion emerges as a tool to alleviate existential dread, presenting narratives of eternal life, reincarnation, or spiritual continuity. For many individuals, such belief systems provide not only comfort but also a vital framework through which to derive meaning beyond the physical realm.

While religious belief satisfies emotional and social needs, scientific thinking demands discomfort. It requires the acceptance of uncertainty, the rejection of intuitive explanations, and the continual questioning of perceived knowledge. Where religion urges belief, science insists on doubt. One offers comfort; the other imposes scrutiny. If belief is intuitive, science is counterintuitive. Science not only fails to satisfy the emotional impulses that religion addresses, but it often undermines them. Science is cognitively demanding and emotionally unsatisfying because it usually conflicts with many of the brain's default settings. Specifically, those for survival, social cohesion, and emotional stability. This is hard to adapt because the brain craves certainty. Emotionally, this can feel hollow, especially compared to the warmth of belief in divine purpose or an afterlife. Science is emotionally unsatisfying and often counterintuitive, unlike the intuitive ease of belief. Much of science runs against common sense or instinct. For example, time isn't absolute—it dilates with speed and gravity, or the Earth feels stationary—but it's spinning at 1,000 mph. These ideas require mental effort to grasp and accept. They don't come naturally in the way that a God made the world might.

Science is descriptive, not prescriptive. It offers no moral compass, no meaning beyond survival and entropy. The universe has no inherent goal or purpose, and it will eventually die in heat death. That's a bleak emotional outlook compared to the promises of eternal life, cosmic justice, or reincarnation offered by various religions. Science, at its best, is not just a method for uncovering facts; it's a lens that reveals the staggering complexity and elegance of the universe. Carl Sagan once wrote, "We are a way for the Cosmos to know itself." This isn't a doctrine, it's poetry rooted in physics. Yet, despite its lack of comfort, individuals continue to devote their lives to science. Why? Because it offers something that belief cannot: not merely answers, but truth. Not just narratives, but the opportunity to participate in the unfolding story of existence. The meaning lies not inherently within the universe, but within the pursuit to understand it. For many, that pursuit becomes sacred, a rebellion against ignorance, a declaration that even in a cold, indifferent cosmos, the human mind will strive to know.

Both advancements in science and religion offer meaningful insights into human experience. The choice between intuitive beliefs and empirical data often comes down to intellectual understanding or ignorance. For instance, there is evidence that dopamine and serotonin are neurochemicals associated with feelings of peace, connection, and euphoria. These chemicals aren't exclusive to religious experiences; they also flourish in the minds of individuals like Carl Sagan, who found peace and wonder in the vastness of the universe. This suggests that the chemical 'rush' often attributed to religious experiences can also be attained through critical thinking and the pursuit of knowledge. However, the tension between intuitive beliefs and empirical data is not just about the search for peace or euphoria; it's also a deeper philosophical divide. Intuitive beliefs, often shaped by culture, upbringing, and personal experiences, can provide individuals with a sense of certainty and comfort, as stated before. They offer answers that feel deeply personal and often unshakable. On the other hand, empirical data requires an openness to uncertainty, a willingness to question what is known, and the humility to accept that knowledge evolves over time.

While intuitive beliefs are rooted in personal experience, they can sometimes bypass critical analysis, leading to a form of intellectual complacency. Empirical data, in contrast, demands rigorous examination and skepticism. This makes it a tool for intellectual growth, yet it can also be perceived as cold or impersonal. The struggle, then, is not just between religion and science, but between two ways of approaching truth: one that is anchored in the subjective, and another that is grounded in the objective. Understanding this divide is key to navigating the complexities of human knowledge and belief.

While the tension between science and belief is often portrayed as a philosophical debate, at its core, it is about the individual's relationship to knowledge. The rejection of science, particularly in the face of overwhelming evidence, can often be traced back to intellectual ignorance or a lack of intellectual understanding. This ignorance is not merely a lack of information, but also a resistance to engaging with or comprehending new ideas that challenge one's existing worldview. Cognitive dissonance plays a key role in this process. When confronted with scientific truths that conflict with personal beliefs, such as climate change, evolution, or vaccines, individuals may experience profound psychological discomfort. Rather than confronting this discomfort by updating their beliefs, they may choose to reject the evidence to maintain a sense of consistency, comfort, and stability in their worldview.

A clear example of this can be seen in the denial of climate change. Despite overwhelming scientific consensus and observable environmental changes, many individuals reject the reality or severity of climate change. This resistance is not due to a lack of access to information, but rather a reluctance to confront truths that might demand uncomfortable changes, whether in personal lifestyle, political identity, or cultural norms. The same mechanism is at play in anti-vaccine movements, where deeply held beliefs about bodily autonomy, distrust in institutions, or anecdotal experiences override decades of scientific research and public health data. In both cases, the tension between faith and evidence is resolved not through reconciliation but through willful ignorance. This reveals how the mind often prioritizes psychological stability over empirical truth.

Moreover, the intellectual disengagement from scientific reasoning is often compounded by a lack of education or access to quality information. Without the tools to critically assess data, people may find it easier to rely on intuitive, informal beliefs rather than engaging with the more complex or abstract concepts offered by science. This is especially true in areas where scientific ideas are not widely understood or are intentionally obscured by misinformation.

The consequences of such intellectual ignorance are profound. It perpetuates division, reinforces ignorance, and stunts societal progress. While science offers the potential to solve some of humanity's most significant challenges, including health crises and climate change, intellectual ignorance stands in the way of solutions. As society continues to advance, it must prioritize the development of intellectual curiosity and critical thinking, tools that can bridge the gap between intuition and empirical data.

Not to say that one couldn't argue and have scientists convinced that religion is where poetry, morals, fashion, art, and so on originated. All of which are society's beneficial contributions, if deemed the result of religion. One will never see progressions in antibiotics or cancer research from the intuitive belief that a God put upon an individual or community.

These progressions in these fields stem from the results and failures of grounding objectives.

Belief without evidence may not be a choice but simply a byproduct of human evolution. Deeply embedded in the human mind, crafted not for truth but for survival. The brain was not built to decipher reality with precision but to cling to familiarity, to see meaning where there is none, and to assign agency to the wind, the stars, or a sudden shadow. Religion, mythology, and superstition did not invade the mind but merely emerged naturally from it. They offered stories to fill the unknown, rituals to ease the chaos, and Gods to answer the silence. And most accepted them, not out of malice, but because belief felt good. It soothed the pain of not knowing and allowed comfort in reality.

Still, comfort is not a measure of truth. Truth is not gentle; it does not cradle the heart. It is dense, indifferent, and solitary. It carries no promises, only clarity. Clarity, for most, is a burden. And so, when the rational mind begins to ask too many questions, it risks being cast out. Socrates was made to drink poison, Galileo was silenced, and Darwin was ridiculed. The price of knowledge is exile, from the collective comfort of shared illusions, from the safety of the herd. Every meaningful discovery, from penicillin to particle physics, was born from doubt, not devotion. The irony is that the comfort of belief is often enjoyed by those who owe their survival methods to the methods they deny.

The divide endures. On one side, a species kneels, eyes closed, wrapped in stories as old as language. On the other, a few stand upright, eyes open, facing the terrifying indifference of the universe. In that silence, they find no Gods but only forces, equations, particles, and questions. But also, a different kind of beauty. Not the sentimental comfort of certainty, but the raw sublime awe of what is. Reaching that place is not about finding comfort but earning clarity. And in a world lulled by illusion, the pursuit of truth remains the loneliest rebellion.

2

Belief in the Age of Evidence

Throughout history, humanity has contemplated an age-old question: Can faith and reason coexist, or are their futures only set for conflict? From theological debates of the medieval period to scientific revolutions of the Enlightenment, the struggle to balance belief and logic has helped shape philosophy, religion, and even the very fabric of human society. For some, faith in the divine has been regarded as an absolute truth that transcends the need for rational explanation. For others, reason grounded in empirical evidence has become the sole factor for determining what is true.

Rather than being inherently contradictory, faith and reason can complement one another, offering distinct perspectives that, when integrated, provide a richer and more nuanced understanding of the natural world and the more profound existential questions that lie beyond it.

As the relationship between faith and reason is explored, the approaches of thinkers from religious and scientific traditions to this intersection will be examined, whether through harmonious collaboration or the sharp edges of their conflict. From the early Church Fathers who sought to reconcile Greek philosophy with Christian doctrine, to the modern-day debates over the compatibility of evolution and creationism, this chapter will examine how faith and reason have both clashed and converged in the pursuit of truth.

When choosing what to believe, one must examine the structure of the sentence presented. For instance, "I believe that Albert Einstein was a person" and "I believe in God". What is the difference between these two statements? In the first statement, "I believe that Albert Einstein was a person," the word "that" is used after the phrase "I believe." This implies that the person who made this statement is either correct or incorrect. Using "I believe that" involves making specific claims that are either true or false. This has more to do with reason, as one can bring evidence to bear. One knows Albert Einstein was real because of many photographs, film footage, written works, and publications. This is all evidence that can be brought to support the statement "I believe that Albert Einstein was a person". However, "I believe in God" carries layers of complexity that go far beyond a simple declaration of faith. This carries a sense of ambiguity: The sentence can go in two directions. The first direction is one's belief that God exists, and the other is one making God a vital part of their life.

The statement "I believe in God" carries an inherent duality that makes it far more complex than a straightforward declaration of belief. On one level, it can be interpreted as a claim of existence—that is, the speaker is asserting that a divine being exists in reality. This is the propositional aspect of the belief, analogous to saying "I believe that gravity exists" or "I believe that Albert Einstein was a real person." In this interpretation, the belief becomes subject to scrutiny, evidence, and argument. One could ask: What reasons do you have for believing that God exists? The conversation would then shift toward rational inquiry, evidence, historical documentation, philosophical arguments (such as the cosmological or teleological), or even personal experiences that the believer may see as proof.

However, this is only one layer of the phrase. The second, perhaps more profound layer, reflects a personal or existential commitment. When someone says, "I believe in God," they may express something closer to trust, hope, or devotion. Here, the word "in" signals not just acceptance of an idea, but a relational stance: a willingness to orient one's life around a divine presence or purpose. It becomes a matter of identity and moral compass. This kind of belief doesn't demand empirical proof like the first; it operates in the domain of faith, meaning, and values, often resisting the binary of true or false. It's not just about what the person thinks is real; it's about what they live for, what gives them strength, and what guides their actions.

This dual nature is essential because it reveals why religious belief can be deeply held and resistant to counterevidence. The first layer might be debated or dismissed on logical grounds, but the second is felt and lived; it provides a foundation for existential stability, moral orientation, and community. It does not merely challenge an idea but often questions someone's entire framework for understanding suffering, purpose, or hope. This is why religious belief persists even in the face of increasing scientific explanations for natural phenomena.

Throughout history, this dual-layered understanding of belief has shaped the lives and legacies of theologians, scientists, and philosophers. Some have viewed faith and reason as opposing forces, while others have worked to integrate them in pursuit of a greater truth.

Saint Augustine of Hippo was a theologian and philosopher of the 4th century. He was among the first to assert that reason and faith could coexist. He believed that human reason was a divine gift meant to guide one to a deeper understanding of God. Before converting to Christianity, Augustine was immersed in the classical traditions of Greek philosophy, particularly Neoplatonism, as well as the Manichaean religion, which emphasized a strict dualism between good and evil. His exposure to such diverse systems of thought laid the groundwork for his later attempts to harmonize reason and revelation. Augustine wrote, "I believe in order to understand, and I understand in order to believe." For Augustine, reason was not the enemy of faith, but instead its indispensable partner. He believed that faith served as the necessary foundation upon which understanding could be built. In Augustine's view, faith opens the door to truths that reason alone cannot grasp, especially regarding metaphysical and spiritual realities.

In sharp contrast to Augustine's harmonious vision of faith and reason, Friedrich Nietzsche stands as one of the most potent critics of religion and its compatibility with rational inquiry. Where Augustine saw belief as the starting point for deeper understanding, Nietzsche saw belief (particularly religious belief) as the very antithesis of reason. To him, faith was not a stepping stone to truth, but a barrier to it. Nietzsche viewed religious faith as a form of intellectual surrender, a retreat from the complex and often uncomfortable pursuit of truth through reason. In The *Antichrist*, he writes with characteristic intensity: "Faith means not wanting to know what is true." This statement captures Nietzsche's central argument: that belief, especially in the context of organized religion, requires the rejection of evidence, inquiry, and doubt. The rejection of evidence, inquiry, and doubt are essentially the fundamental tools for reason.

Nietzsche saw Christianity in particular as life-denying, built on guilt, submission, and the promise of an afterlife that robbed meaning from this one. He believed that religious systems often arose not from an honest search for truth but from psychological needs:

The need to explain the unknown, stability, the fear of suffering, and the desire for control. In this view, faith is not interlinked with reason but a result of weakness, a refusal to confront the chaos and complexity of life head-on.

He famously declared that "God is dead", now modernized as a metaphorical expression describing the collapse of traditional religious frameworks. This worldview culminated in Nietzsche's concept of the Übermensch (or "Overman"), an individual who creates meaning through willpower, not divine revelation. The Übermensch is unafraid of uncertainty, unburdened by inherited dogma, and guided by the courage to live without absolutes. In Nietzsche, one finds the extreme counterpoint to Augustine: a worldview in which reason does not serve belief but liberates humanity from it. This radical perspective raises profound questions. What is lost when belief is abandoned, and conversely, what might be gained when the world is confronted through reason alone?

Having outlined Nietzsche's fundamental critique of belief, it is crucial to consider the societal consequences of abandoning belief altogether. For some, their sense of meaning and purpose. Not that one cannot find a sense of meaning without belief, for instance, the Übermensch mentioned in the last paragraph, but belief systems often give people a sense of why they exist, their role, and how to live. The narratives that belief provides help people make sense of suffering, death, and the unknown. For others, it's their community and belonging. Religion, for example, often builds networks of support that extend across generations. These networks serve as more than places of worship; they act as community pillars offering food banks, childcare, elder care, job placement services, and scholarship opportunities. Within their walls, families are supported through every stage of life, from birth to death, with traditions and values passed down through generations. Elders mentor the youth, young adults care for the aging, and spiritual guidance is woven into the community's everyday needs. This continuity fosters a deep sense of identity and belonging that has an impact that outlives individual lifespans, creating a cultural and emotional fabric that is difficult to replicate through secular means alone. To be clear, the abandonment of belief does not necessarily entail the loss of meaning, community, or ritual. However, unless intentional efforts are made to reconstruct these elements through secular or alternative frameworks, the absence of belief can result in real and tangible losses. While science offers explanations for how the world works, belief systems have traditionally provided the why—a sense of purpose, direction, and existential coherence. In the absence of these frameworks, society must seek new narratives and new forms of community to fill the void left behind.

Yet while the loss of belief may deprive society of meaning and community, turning fully toward reason offers its own distinct set of potential gains. Society stands to gain a more calculated and efficient means of progressing both practical and philosophical challenges. Using reason, all decision-making becomes rooted in evidence, logic, and reproducibility. When this happens, it will reduce the influence of superstition, dogma, and emotionally guided misinformation. When the world is confronted through reason alone, scientific and technological progress may accelerate under this example. Historically, the Enlightenment is a compelling example of a time when increased rational thought led to advances in medicine, physics, and political theory. The eradication of diseases such as smallpox, the formulation of modern democratic institutions, and the industrial revolution all emerged from a growing reliance on empirical methodologies and reasoned debate.

Only in a reason-centered society are ethical systems to evolve along utilitarian lines, prioritizing outcomes that maximize well-being and minimize harm. Effective altruism reflects this rationalist ethos by urging individuals and organizations to use evidence-based strategies to achieve the greatest good. Legal frameworks and public policy could be increasingly shaped by measurable outcomes rather than tradition or religious morality, seen in initiatives such as data-driven criminal justice reforms aimed at reducing relapse, or behavioral science applications in designing public health interventions. Rational discourse can potentially foster a culture of open inquiry and intellectual humility. In such a society, ideological divides may be bridged through structured dialogue based on shared facts and logical coherence. Deliberative democracy, where citizens engage in informed discussions before making policy decisions, exemplifies a rational approach to governance that prioritizes reasoned consensus over partisan division.

However, a society grounded purely in reason is not without its own limitations, particularly when addressing human beings' emotional and existential needs. While this provides clarity and control over the physical world, it often struggles to address the emotional, existential, and symbolic dimensions of human life. Emotionally, people seek comfort and expression and grapple with questions of purpose, identity, and mortality, questions like "Why am I here?" or "What happens when I die?" that cannot be answered through empirical evidence alone. Symbolically, humans create meaning through rituals, myths, and cultural symbols that represent values, beliefs, and shared histories. Logic may explain the neurochemical basis of grief, but it cannot soothe the pain of loss in the same way that ritual, narrative, or spiritual belief can. Technologies born from rational innovation may increase connectivity, yet still leave individuals feeling isolated, as efficiency and optimization overshadow empathy and human warmth. For example, mental health cognitive-behavioral therapy is an evidence-based, rational approach that has proven effective for many. Yet others find healing through spiritual practices, communal rituals, or belief systems that offer a sense of purpose and transcendence. Another question that would put a close to this plot hole is "would these solutions, such as spiritual practices, communal rituals, or belief systems, even exist or be a solution in a world truly ruled by reason?" This is asked in the assumption that the opposition of this world of reason is "some people find purpose in belief systems, so a world of reason couldn't fill the void of human meaning". If it were truly a world of reason, then that question wouldn't pose meaning due to "belief in" statements not existing. It's like the most famous analogy of questions like this: "What's north of the north pole?". The North Pole is defined as the northernmost point on Earth. All lines of longitude converge there; by definition, there is no direction "north" of it; it's the top of the planet geographically. One could argue that in a world of strict reason, society may need a tool such as belief to fulfil specific meaning in life. Yet, it is intriguing to entertain the notion of "belief being a solution" as not existing in a world of just reason.

In contemporary society, the tension between faith and reason shapes public discourse, particularly in debates surrounding evolution and creationism. While scientific evidence overwhelmingly supports the theory of evolution, certain religious communities persist in teaching creationism as an alternative explanation for the origins of life. Similarly, the rapid advancement of artificial intelligence raises profound ethical questions, which require both rational inquiry and moral consideration. These ongoing debates highlight the complexities of balancing reason with belief in a world increasingly defined by scientific discovery.

Looking ahead, the connection between faith and reason may undergo a notable transformation. As global society is becoming increasingly secular, it's possible that faith and reason will need to find a new way to coexist. This is especially true with shared global challenges such as climate change, artificial intelligence, and genetic engineering. There are three broad models for the future: Integration, Parallelism, and Conflict. What does it mean for faith and reason to coexist and integrate? Integration model-Harmonization of faith and reason, suggesting they can inform and enrich each other towards a more holistic view of reality.

Historically, prominent figures have sought this harmony. Thomas Aquinas in the 13th century famously argued that there could be no ultimate conflict between faith and reason because both originate from the same divine source. According to Aquinas, natural reason could lead one to many truths about the universe, including the existence of God, while divine revelation completed and perfected the knowledge that reason alone could not fully achieve. Similarly, during the Islamic Golden Age, thinkers like Averroes and Al-Farabi emphasized that philosophy and religion, properly understood, were different paths toward the same truth. In Jewish thought, Maimonides sought to interpret the Torah through the lens of Aristotelian philosophy, arguing that apparent contradictions between reason and revelation stemmed from misunderstandings.

In contemporary times, this integrative spirit persists. Figures like Francis Collins, a renowned geneticist and devout Christian, see no contradiction between their scientific work and religious faith. Collins has argued that scientific discovery enhances his awe of creation, deepening his spiritual beliefs rather than diminishing them. Although this is only one case representing a very small percentage of geneticists and biologists who do not see a problem with religious text and reason harmonizing, it should still be recognized and attributed to the integration model. The same model that demands a careful balance: if faith attempts to dictate empirical truths without evidence, it risks devolving into dogmatism; if reason dismisses all non-empirical knowledge as irrational, it risks becoming scientism (a worldview that acknowledges only what can be quantified), overlooking the richness of human experience. Proper integration requires a willingness to engage in dialogue, live with tension, and respect each domain's legitimate insights.

Another prominent way of conceptualizing the relationship between faith and reason is through the separation model. Rather than viewing them as allies seeking harmony, this model suggests that faith and reason operate in fundamentally distinct domains, each with its own questions, methods, and authorities. In this perspective, reason (embodied by the sciences and philosophy) concerns empirical realities: what the universe is made of, how it functions, and what can be measured, tested, and predicted. In contrast, faith deals with questions beyond empirical scrutiny: the purpose of existence, the foundation of moral values, and the search for ultimate meaning. Each domain is self-contained; ideally, neither should encroach upon the other.

One of the most influential advocates of a separation between faith and reason was philosopher Immanuel Kant. In his Critique of Pure Reason, Kant argued that human knowledge is limited to phenomena, the world as it appears through sensory experience and rational analysis—questions about God's existence, the soul's immortality, and the ultimate purpose of life. Kant's beliefs belong to noumena (realities that lie beyond empirical observation and rational proof). Thus, while science can investigate the natural world through reason and experimentation, matters of faith must be approached through moral reasoning and practical necessity, rather than theoretical knowledge. In Kant's view, reason and faith serve distinct but complementary purposes, and conflict arises only when one tries to overstep into the other's domain. Maintaining distinct boundaries reduces the likelihood of unnecessary conflict: religious faith does not interfere with scientific progress, and scientific discoveries are not misused to affirm or deny theological doctrines. Each domain can flourish according to its own methods and standards, preserving the integrity of empirical investigation and spiritual reflection.

However, both sides risk the potential of inadvertently losing insight or company. This applies to ethical questions that arise from scientific discoveries like genetic engineering. Discoveries like genetic engineering often require moral frameworks to guide action, and many are rooted in religious traditions. Likewise, religious claims about the origins of life, human nature, or destiny can sometimes overlap with scientific inquiries, creating tensions that the separation model struggles to address fully.

The separation model is supposed to represent an effort to broker peace between two powerful human impulses: the drive to understand the world through rational inquiry and the yearning to find meaning and moral direction. Though it does not eliminate all tensions between faith and reason, it provides a framework for coexistence—a pragmatic truce that allows each to contribute, in its own way, to the broader human pursuit of knowledge, purpose, and wisdom.

While some thinkers view science and religion as irreconcilable, others argue that they are not competing systems but complementary ones. For example, after centuries of resistance, the Catholic Church has come to embrace aspects of modern science, especially in the field of cosmology. Georges Lemaître, a Catholic priest and physicist, is one of the most prominent examples of someone who saw no conflict between his faith and scientific work. His development of the Big Bang theory exemplified how scientific inquiry and religious belief could coexist in a framework that respected the pursuit of empirical evidence and spiritual understanding. Today, many see science as a means of exploring the divine, using scientific discoveries to deepen their appreciation for the mystery of existence.

Some have sought integration or separation between faith and reason; others have argued that the two are fundamentally incompatible, locked in an inevitable and ongoing conflict. This conflict model proposes that religious faith and scientific reason make competing claims about reality, and these claims often directly contradict one another. Rather than representing different domains of human inquiry, faith and reason are seen as rival systems vying for authority over the same questions.

One prominent advocate of the conflict model was Andrew Dickson White, a 19th-century historian and co-founder of Cornell University. In his influential work *A History of the Warfare of Science with Theology in Christendom* (1896), White argued that the relationship between science and religion was largely one of open hostility. He documented numerous historical cases, from opposition to heliocentrism (mentioned earlier) to resistance against vaccination, portraying religion as a persistent obstacle to scientific advancement. For White, the progress of human knowledge depended on freeing science from the constraints of theological authority. His writings helped cement the popular narrative of an enduring "warfare" between faith and reason, even though later historians would criticize his account for exaggerating the intensity and simplicity of this conflict.

More recently, proponents such as Richard Dawkins have renewed the conflict model with renewed vigor. In *The God Delusion*, Dawkins argues that religious belief is not just irrational but harmful, standing in the way of scientific progress and fostering intolerance. He sees faith as "a delusion" precisely because it demands acceptance without evidence, the antithesis of scientific reasoning, which thrives on doubt, testing, and the willingness to revise one's beliefs based on new information. Much of which was mentioned in the previous chapter.

While Richard Dawkins strongly critiques religion, other thinkers, such as Carl Sagan, found a sense of wonder in the scientific exploration of the universe, which he viewed as rational and awe-inspiring. Sagan argued that the quest for knowledge through science does not diminish the mystery of existence but enhances it, inviting a deep sense of reverence for the Cosmos without resorting to supernatural explanations.

The conflict model highlights dramatic historical moments where religious and scientific authorities clashed: Galileo's condemnation by the Catholic Church, the Scopes Trial over teaching evolution in

American schools, and contemporary debates over vaccines or climate change policy shaped by religious ideologies. In each case, defenders of reason and science have portrayed religious belief as an obstacle to knowledge and human flourishing.

Critics of the conflict model argue that it oversimplifies a much more complex historical and philosophical relationship. They emphasize that some of the greatest scientific minds, such as Isaac Newton, Gregor Mendel, and Georges Lemaître, were deeply religious and saw no contradiction between their faith and scientific work. Moreover, religious institutions, including the Catholic Church, have historically funded astronomical observatories, universities, and scientific research initiatives. Rather than being purely adversarial, the relationship between science and religion has often been one of mutual influence, cooperation, and even inspiration. Despite these nuances, the conflict model remains a powerful and enduring narrative, particularly in a modern world where rapid scientific advances, some of which are mentioned earlier, genetic engineering, evolution, artificial intelligence, and cosmology, continue to unsettle traditional religious explanations about life, morality, and the fundamental nature of the universe. In this view, science and religion are locked in a perpetual struggle for authority over truth, each challenging the other's claims to explain reality and human purpose.

While the historical tension between faith and reason played out through debates about heliocentrism, evolution, and vaccination, today's technological revolution brings new challenges. Emerging fields like artificial intelligence pose questions about life, consciousness, and human nature that echo ancient theological dilemmas. In this way, the conflict and separation between faith and reason are not simply relics of the past but continue to evolve in response to modern developments.

Artificial intelligence presents some of the most profound challenges and opportunities in this reimagining of belief affecting reason. As AI systems grow more sophisticated, the line between machine computation and human cognition becomes increasingly blurred. When machines can mimic human conversation, solve complex problems, and even generate art or scientific theories, questions arise about the nature of intelligence, consciousness, and self-awareness. AI learns from large datasets, like teaching children to solve problems or recognize patterns. Imagine teaching a child how to identify a cat by showing them thousands of pictures of cats.

Similarly, an AI system is trained to recognize patterns in data. Some futurists speculate about the eventual emergence of artificial general intelligence, a machine with cognitive abilities equal to or surpassing those of humans. Such a possibility provokes existential and spiritual questions: If a machine becomes self-aware, does it possess a soul? Can it have rights? Can humans create "life" in a way once thought to be the exclusive domain of divine power? In these debates, belief is no longer tethered solely to ancient religious traditions but is being reformulated to grapple with the unprecedented realities of the technological age.

This redefinition of belief in the age of AI forces a broader reconsideration of what it means to trust and to attribute authority. As societies increasingly interact with algorithms that recommend life decisions, diagnose illnesses, and even create art or journalism, belief is shifting away from traditional human institutions toward the hidden mechanisms of code and machine learning. Much like conventional religions required faith in the unseen and the mysterious, modern reliance on technology demands a new kind of trust — one rooted not in divine revelation, but in the presumed reliability of technological systems. Some scholars have warned about the spiritual consequences of this shift; as theologian Michael Burdett notes, "If artificial intelligence were to achieve consciousness, it would fundamentally destabilize the theological concept of humanity's unique place in creation." Such concerns raise urgent ethical and philosophical questions: Who designs these systems, and with what biases? What happens when technology fails, misleads, or develops goals misaligned with human values? As AI becomes more deeply embedded into the fabric of everyday life, it blurs the boundaries between belief, reason, and trust, revealing a future where traditional frameworks may no longer be sufficient to answer humanity's most profound existential questions. In this new frontier, belief and reason may no longer be adversaries from different traditions but evolving forces intertwined in co-creating the future.

The ongoing tension between belief and evidence represents more than just an intellectual debate; it stands as a fundamental contest for how humanity will confront the unknown. On one side, belief in the supernatural has long served as a source of comfort and explanation, offering solace to those who grapple with existence's uncertainties. It provides a sense of meaning in an otherwise chaotic world and promises answers to life's most profound questions. But is this belief merely a comforting illusion, or does it serve a deeper, more vital function for human beings, one that science, with all its rational clarity, cannot fulfill?

One might argue that faith, at its core, is a human necessity, woven into the fabric of culture and society. Perhaps belief in the unseen gives life purpose and guides moral behavior, especially when empirical evidence is inaccessible or irrelevant. Faith-based explanations of the world may offer a sense of security to many, allowing them to navigate the unpredictability of existence without relying on the cold, harsh realism of scientific inquiry. From this standpoint, it could be contended that belief in God or the supernatural has provided countless individuals with a framework for understanding suffering, morality, and the afterlife—questions that science offers no definitive answers to.

However, when examined under the lens of modern science, the persistence of faith in the supernatural becomes less palatable. The claims of religion, unsubstantiated by evidence, have been tested and found wanting. As Richard Dawkins often points out, belief in the divine is not grounded in the rationality or critical thinking that underpins scientific discovery. Instead, it relies on tradition, authority, and an emotional yearning for certainty, traits that often do not hold up when scrutinized through the lens of reason and empirical investigation. To believe without evidence is to abandon the very principles of inquiry that have propelled humanity to its most significant accomplishments.

In this light, the persistence of faith, despite its inability to provide verifiable truth, is a form of intellectual laziness or an avoidance of the uncomfortable yet liberating responsibility to confront the world as it truly is. Though imperfect and incomplete, science has consistently provided humanity with answers to questions once dominated by mythology and superstition. It has unlocked the secrets of the universe, illuminated life processes, and revealed the true nature of human existence (all without recourse to divine intervention or supernatural explanations). The remarkable achievements of science, from medicine to technology, have shown that reality, though often harsh and unforgiving, offers more profound meaning than any religious narrative can provide.

Still, one must acknowledge that belief in the supernatural is not easily vanquished. It remains deeply ingrained in human culture, with many finding meaning in practices and doctrines that offer emotional support in times of crisis. While science continues to provide insights into the mechanics of the universe, it struggles to address the more profound existential questions that drive human motivation and behavior. Is it possible that belief, even without evidence, serves a necessary psychological function that science, in its relentless pursuit of truth, cannot fulfill?

It is here that the role of reason and skepticism becomes critical. While it can be argued that belief provides comfort, this alone is insufficient justification for clinging to ideas that distort reality. As Dawkins and others have emphasized, the consequences of unchallenged belief can be far-reaching, fueling dogma, intolerance, and a resistance to the progress that has led humanity out of the dark ages. Only through skepticism, critical thinking, and the relentless pursuit of evidence can humanity continue to move forward, challenging outdated beliefs and confronting the unknown with intellectual honesty.

The question is not whether belief has a place in human life; It certainly does, in a cultural and psychological sense, but whether it should continue to dominate humanity's understanding of the world. Faith, though deeply ingrained in human history, is not a reliable guide to truth. The future of society must be built on a foundation of reason, scientific inquiry, and a willingness to face the discomfort of uncertainty, rather than retreat into the comforting arms of superstition. If humanity is to thrive, it must reject the delusions of faith and embrace the uncomfortable clarity of evidence, no matter where it may lead

3

What Remains After Genesis

It is one thing to say, "How can people not believe in evolution when there is proof for it?" but it is another to actually understand and present that proof. Many people accept evolution based on the testimony of scientists, especially biologists, rather than on personal familiarity with the evidence itself. This reliance on expert consensus is not inherently problematic—after all, science functions as a collaborative enterprise built on trust in expertise. However, it becomes ironic when individuals criticize religious belief for lacking evidence, while defending evolution without understanding its scientific basis.

The evidence for evolution stems from every branch of science that remotely interacts with organisms. This includes botany, ecology, zoology, anatomy, mycology, microbiology, and many more. This chapter aims to clarify some of the key lines of evidence for evolution in a way accessible to those without a background in biology. It will also explore how specific religious interpretations can coexist with evolutionary theory and how other belief systems reject that compatibility. While the whole body of evolutionary evidence spans countless disciplines and could fill volumes, this chapter will focus on a few striking and comprehensible examples. The goal is to bridge the knowledge gap between scientific understanding and everyday belief, creating a better-informed perspective on evolution.

One of the clearest ways to see evolution in action is to examine structures in the human body that seem oddly designed. These features make sense not through intelligent planning, but as inherited byproducts of evolutionary change. A notable example is the path of the left recurrent laryngeal nerve. The nerve branches from the vagus nerve in the chest, looping under the aortic arch before ascending alongside the trachea and esophagus to reach the larynx. This nerve controls most of the intrinsic muscles of the larynx and provides sensory input below the vocal cords, making it essential for voice production and airway protection. Although the nerve's functional destination, the larynx, is located only a few inches from the brain, the nerve takes a long and seemingly inefficient path. It descends deep into the chest, wraps around a major artery (the aortic arch), and then travels back up to the neck. This detour becomes especially extreme in giraffes, stretching the nerve over fifteen feet longer than a direct route would require. Richard Dawkins famously described this anatomical arrangement as "a mistake that no engineer would ever make," highlighting its inefficiency from a design perspective. However, routing the nerve around the artery is structurally logical in neckless animals such as fish due to their compact body plans. This long path of the left recurrent laryngeal nerve being the most efficient path leads to a safe assumption that if mammals evolved from a fishlike creature, it would make sense why this nerve takes such a long, inefficient detour.

Just as physical anatomy can reveal evolutionary patterns, so can the molecular structures inside our cells. DNA sequencing has become one of the most valuable tools for tracing evolutionary relationships. All living organisms use the same basic genetic code, strongly suggesting a common origin. Researchers can identify similarities and differences in genes across species by analyzing the sequences of nucleotides (adenine, thymine, cytosine, and guanine). These comparisons have revealed that closely related organisms share a higher percentage of identical sequences. For example, humans and chimpanzees share about 98 to 99 percent of their DNA, indicating that they diverged from a common ancestor relatively recently in evolutionary terms. More distantly related species, such as humans and chickens, share fewer similarities, but still possess many conserved genes, especially those responsible for fundamental biological processes. DNA also contains "molecular fossils" such as pseudogenes, which are nonfunctional remnants of once-active genes. These pseudogenes appear in similar forms across related species, further supporting shared ancestry.

Additionally, scientists can track inherited mutations across generations, constructing genetic family trees that align closely with evolutionary trees based on fossil and anatomical evidence. This genetic continuity across all life forms provides a clear, measurable, and predictive framework for understanding how species have evolved over millions of years. DNA sequencing confirms evolutionary theory and enables scientists to estimate divergence times and trace the historical relationships between all forms of life on Earth.

Evolution can also be observed on shorter timescales, which is known as microevolution. Microevolution refers to small-scale evolutionary changes that occur within a population over a relatively short period of time. It involves changes in the frequency of specific alleles (genetic variations) in a population due to natural selection, genetic drift, mutation, and gene flow. These changes can affect traits such as size, color, or resistance to disease. For example, when a population of organisms faces environmental changes, those with advantageous traits are more likely to survive and reproduce, passing on their genes to the next generation. Over time, these changes accumulate, leading to noticeable shifts in the population's genetic makeup. Microevolution demonstrates how species can adapt to their environment, often without forming a new species.

An example of microevolution is the development of antibiotic resistance in bacteria. Antibiotics are designed to kill or inhibit the growth of bacteria by either being bactericidal or bacteriostatic, targeting specific processes, such as cell wall synthesis, like penicillin, or protein production, like tetracyclines.

However, when an antibiotic is introduced to a population of bacteria, it eliminates most of the bacteria, leaving behind a small subset that may have mutations conferring resistance. These mutations, occurring naturally in the bacterial DNA, allow the resistant bacteria to survive the antibiotic treatment and reproduce. As a result, the resistant bacteria pass their resistance traits to their offspring, gradually increasing the proportion of resistant bacteria in the population.

Over time, this process shifts the genetic makeup of the bacterial population, a clear example of natural selection at work. The bacteria with resistance mutations have a survival advantage and are more likely to reproduce, while the non-resistant bacteria are killed off. In environments where antibiotics are heavily used, such as hospitals or agricultural settings, the selective pressure for resistant bacteria is even greater, accelerating the process. One notable example of this phenomenon is Methicillin-resistant *Staphylococcus aureus* (MRSA), a strain of bacteria that has evolved resistance to many common antibiotics, making it more challenging to treat. Additionally, these genetic resistance traits can spread rapidly through a process known as horizontal gene transfer, where resistant genes are shared between different bacterial species. This exchange further amplifies the spread of resistance across bacterial populations.

In this way, the development of antibiotic resistance illustrates microevolution, where genetic changes in a population occur quickly due to environmental pressures. It serves as a reminder of how evolution operates in real-time, emphasizing the importance of responsible antibiotic use to slow the spread of resistance and maintain the effectiveness of current treatments.

While microevolution refers to small genetic shifts within populations, macroevolution refers to large-scale evolutionary changes that occur over long periods, including the formation of new species and major biological groups. These changes are built upon the gradual accumulation of genetic variation and adaptations seen in microevolution, just extended across millions of years. One of the most powerful lines of evidence for macroevolution is the fossil record, which preserves a historical sequence of life on Earth. Although not every organism becomes fossilized, the record still reveals key transitions in evolutionary history. Among the most informative fossils are transitional forms. These fossils show traits shared between ancestral and modern species, helping scientists trace how one group gradually evolved into another, one of the most popular examples being the evolutionary transition of land-dwelling mammals into fully aquatic whales.

Fossils such as *Pakicetus*, *Ambulocetus*, and *Rodhocetus* represent stages in this transformation. *Pakicetus*, which lived about 50 million years ago, had limbs capable of supporting its body on land, but also displayed features of the inner ear that are uniquely found in whales. *Ambulocetus*, often called the "walking whale," likely moved between land and water much like a modern crocodile, using its strong limbs and tail to swim. Later species, such as *Rodhocetus,* became more aquatic, with shorter limbs and a more streamlined body, better suited for swimming. Over time, these intermediate forms evolved into fully aquatic whales, like those we see today. Modern whales still retain vestiges of their terrestrial past, such as tiny pelvic bones that no longer serve a function in locomotion. These fossils provide strong evidence for a gradual transition from land mammals to marine creatures, aligning with evolutionary predictions.

The fossil record offers isolated examples. It reveals broader patterns of species emerging, adapting, and sometimes going extinct in a way that fits the evolutionary model. These patterns allow researchers to reconstruct evolutionary trees and understand how complex features, including aquatic adaptations, developed over time through natural selection.

Another line of evidence for evolution comes from vestigial structures (physical features that have lost most or all of their original function over time). These features are often inherited from ancestors, in which they served a useful purpose, but through changes in environment or behavior, they have become redundant or repurposed. Vestigial traits act like biological footprints, revealing an organism's origin and hinting at its evolutionary past.

In humans, the appendix is often looked at as a vestigial organ. While it may play a minor role in immune function, it is a reduced version of a larger, more complex cecum found in herbivorous ancestors, where it helped digest tough plants. As human diets shifted and reliance on this digestive role diminished, the organ became smaller and less essential. Similarly, the coccyx, or tailbone, is a remnant of a tail present in our distant primate ancestors. Although it now serves as an anchor point for specific muscles, it no longer functions as a tail used for balance or movement.

Other species show even more dramatic vestiges. Whales and some snakes, for instance, possess tiny internal pelvic bones. These bones no longer play a role in locomotion but are remnants of their legged ancestors. Flightless birds like ostriches and emus have wings that are too small for flight, yet these wings are structurally similar to those of birds that do fly. This suggests that these birds evolved from flying ancestors but adapted to life on the ground.

Evolutionary remnants are not only physical. They also appear in our genomes. Pseudogenes are remnants of once-active genes. Sometimes, the identical pseudogenes appear in multiple related species, suggesting a shared ancestry. For example, humans, chimpanzees, and gorillas all share a broken gene for vitamin C synthesis, which functions in other mammals but no longer works in these primates. These features make little sense if each species was designed independently, but they fit perfectly into the evolutionary framework. Vestigial traits provide insight into the history of life, showing how organisms have changed and adapted over time, while still carrying echoes of their evolutionary origins.

While the scientific evidence for evolution is extensive and will only continue to grow, not all worldviews respond to this evidence in the same way.

For many, especially those grounded in religious traditions, evolution raises essential questions about human origins and the interpretation of sacred texts. Some religious perspectives have found ways to reconcile evolution with their spiritual beliefs, seeing science as a means of understanding the mechanisms through which a divine force acts. Others, however, view evolution as fundamentally incompatible with their doctrines, particularly when it contradicts literal readings of creation stories.

The following section will explore how different religions interpret evolution, highlighting both attempts at integration and points of conflict. By examining these perspectives, we can better understand the ongoing conversation between science and faith and why the relationship between the two remains a central topic in public and philosophical discourse.

In Christianity, responses to evolution span a broad spectrum, shaped by varying interpretations of Scripture and theological priorities. Some Christian groups view evolution as a direct challenge to the biblical account of creation, while others see it as a tool through which God expresses divine creativity. Three major perspectives: Young Earth Creationism,

Intelligent Design, and Theistic Evolution, all illustrate this wide range of thought.

At one end of the spectrum is Young Earth Creationism (YEC). This view interprets the Book of Genesis as a literal, historical account, asserting that God created the world and all life in six 24-hour days, approximately 6,000 to 10,000 years ago. YEC advocates often cite specific passages such as "And there was evening and there was morning, the first day" (Genesis 1:5) to argue that the word "day" refers to a literal 24-hour period, not a symbolic or metaphorical era. The sequential structure of the creation narrative—"God made the beasts of the earth after their kind, and the cattle after their kind, and every thing that creepeth upon the earth after his kind" (Genesis 1:25)—is also interpreted as evidence that species were created in fixed forms and did not evolve from one another.

Further, Genesis 1:27 states, "So God created man in his own image, in the image of God created he him; male and female created he them." YEC adherents view this verse as proof that humans were created as distinct beings, separate from the animals, and not the product of evolutionary descent. Advocates of YEC reject much of modern science, including radiometric dating, evolutionary biology, and geology, arguing that these disciplines contradict what they consider to be a biblically faithful understanding of Earth's history. Organizations such as Answers in Genesis advocate for this interpretation and warn that accepting evolutionary theory undermines scriptural authority and may lead to broader theological compromises. In this framework, all living organisms were created in their present form by divine action, and any observable changes within species are considered mere variations within fixed "kinds," rather than evidence of common descent or speciation as described in Darwinian evolution.

A more moderate perspective is Intelligent Design (ID), which accepts the possibility of microevolution but contends that certain features of life are too complex to have arisen through natural selection alone. ID advocates argue that an intelligent cause must be responsible for the intricate structures found in biological systems. Biochemist Michael Behe, one of the most well-known ID advocates, introduced the concept of "irreducible complexity." He claims that some systems, such as the bacterial flagellum, could not function if any of their parts were removed and thus could not have evolved through gradual modifications. Critics of Intelligent Design argue that it lacks empirical support and does not produce testable hypotheses. As a result, the scientific community generally does not accept ID as a legitimate scientific theory, instead viewing it as a rebranded form of creationism.

On the opposite end is Theistic Evolution, also known as evolutionary creationism. This view holds that evolution is the mechanism through which God brought about the diversity of life on Earth. Theistic evolutionists fully accept the findings of modern science, including common ancestry and natural selection, while maintaining that God is the ultimate creator and sustainer of life. Many mainstream Christian denominations endorse this perspective. The Roman Catholic Church, for example, officially recognizes evolution as compatible with Christian faith. In his 1950 encyclical *Humani Generis*, Pope Pius XII stated that there is no inherent conflict between Catholic doctrine and the theory of evolution, as long as the soul is understood to be directly created by God. Later, Pope Benedict XVI affirmed this position, emphasizing that science and faith address different dimensions of human understanding and can coexist harmoniously.

Critics of Theistic Evolution argue that it compromises both the authority of Scripture and the coherence of Christian theology by trying to reconcile fundamentally different worldviews. One of the central concerns is that evolution by natural selection is a process characterized by random mutations, competition, and death, which seems inconsistent with the nature of a purposeful and benevolent Creator. Suppose suffering, extinction, and genetic trial-and-error are God's chosen tools for creating life. In that case, this raises profound theological questions about God's character and the original goodness of creation described in Genesis.

A common objection stems from the narrative of Adam and Eve. Genesis 2:7 states, "Then the Lord God formed man of the dust of the ground, and breathed into his nostrils the breath of life." This direct and intimate act of creation is difficult to reconcile with the idea of human beings arising gradually from non-human ancestors over millions of years. If Adam was not a historical individual, the doctrine of original sin, as described in Romans 5:12 ("Wherefore, as by one man sin entered into the world, and death by sin..."), becomes problematic. Without a literal Fall, the need for redemption through Christ could be undermined, which strikes at the heart of Christian soteriology.

Additionally, critics argue that Theistic Evolution imposes modern scientific interpretations onto ancient religious texts, which were never meant to accommodate such frameworks. Rather than reading Scripture through the lens of contemporary science, they believe Christians should let the Bible interpret itself. Accepting evolution, they argue, risks turning foundational doctrines into allegories, which may lead to reinterpretation where core theological beliefs lose their grounding.

In this view, the harmonious coexistence of science and faith proposed by Theistic Evolution is more of a philosophical ideal than a theological reality. While science offers valuable insights into the physical world, critics maintain that its explanations must not override Scripture's clear teachings regarding the origin, purpose, and dignity of human life.

These three viewpoints (Young Earth Creationism, Intelligent Design, and Theistic Evolution) demonstrate Christianity and science's complex and evolving relationship. While some Christians maintain a strict, literal interpretation of Scripture, others find meaningful ways to integrate scientific knowledge with theological belief. The diversity of views within Christianity highlights an ongoing dialogue that continues to shape how religious communities understand human origins and the nature of life itself.

Beyond Christianity, Islam offers a range of perspectives on evolution, shaped by theological interpretation and differing emphases on literal versus allegorical readings of scripture. While the Qur'an does not explicitly discuss the mechanisms of evolution, it presents a narrative of divine creation that some interpret as flexible enough to accommodate modern science. However, just like in Christianity, interpretations vary dramatically.

Many conservative Muslims reject evolutionary theory, especially regarding human origins, citing verses that emphasize God's direct creation of Adam. For example, Surah 38:71 72 states: "When your Lord said to the angels, 'I am creating a human being from clay, from molded mud. So when I have proportioned him and breathed into him of My spirit, fall down in prostration to him.'" This passage is often taken to affirm the special and direct creation of human beings by Allah, separate from other creatures. In this view, while animals might evolve, humans were uniquely crafted by divine command, not descended from earlier primates.

However, other Muslim scholars adopt more metaphorical interpretations of such verses, suggesting compatibility between the Qur'anic creation narrative and the evolutionary process. Surah

24:45 notes, "Allah created every [living] creature from water." Some interpret this verse as aligning with scientific observations that life originated in aquatic environments. Similarly, verses referring to stages of human creation (from clay, then a drop of fluid, and then a clot) have been read by modern scholars as poetically compatible with embryological and evolutionary development.

This has led to multiple schools of thought within Islamic theology. "Non-exceptionalists" fully embrace evolution, including human evolution, interpreting Adam as a symbolic or spiritual figure. Others, like proponents of "Adamic exceptionalism," accept the evolution of earlier hominins but maintain that Adam and Eve were divinely created as the first true humans. Still others accept the evolution of all life except for humans, citing the Qur'an's insistence on humanity's spiritual and moral uniqueness. The cultural variation is just as wide. Muslims in Turkey, Iran, and the Arab world often view evolution skeptically, while Muslims in countries like Kazakhstan, Lebanon, and parts of the West show significantly greater acceptance.

Islamic scholars today continue to engage this topic. Thinkers like Dr. Shoaib Ahmed Malik and Dr. Yasir QadhI explore the intersection of science and theology, working to reconcile evolutionary theory with Islamic belief without compromising core doctrines. In this ongoing discourse, the Islamic world reflects a similar spectrum seen in Christianity. Ranging from outright rejection to cautious integration to full embrace. This diversity reveals that the relationship between evolution and faith is not determined solely by doctrine but by how religious communities interpret, contextualize, and live out their sacred texts in the face of new knowledge.

Compared to the rigidity of some Western monotheistic traditions, Hinduism presents a much more flexible framework for evolution. That's mainly because Hindu cosmology isn't centered around a single, literal act of creation. Instead, it embraces a cyclical view of the universe, with birth, destruction, and rebirth repeating infinitely. This alone makes room for a worldview that doesn't necessarily feel threatened by evolutionary theory. In fact, for many Hindus, evolution seems like another form of samsara, the ongoing process of change, transformation, and rebirth.

One of the more interesting overlaps between evolutionary thinking and Hindu belief is the story of the Dashavatara, or the ten incarnations of Vishnu. The sequence of avatars begins with Matsya (a fish), then transitions into Kurma (a turtle), a boar, then a half-human creature, and eventually into complete human forms like Krishna and the Buddha. Obviously, it's not presented as science, but the order is strikingly similar to the evolutionary progression of life from aquatic to amphibian to mammal to human. Many Hindus don't see this as a coincidence, but as evidence that their tradition anticipated a form of evolution thousands of years ago through myth.

Hinduism is unique in this conversation because it rarely demands a binary between science and faith. The Rig Veda, one of the oldest known religious texts, literally questions the origins of existence without claiming to know them. One line reads, "Who really knows? Who will here proclaim it? Whence was it produced? Whence is this creation?" The text even concedes that the gods themselves may not know how creation unfolded. That ambiguity allows believers to hold space for uncertainty, mystery, and scientific discovery without tearing down their spiritual foundations.

Because of this openness, many Hindus don't consider evolutionary theory a threat. The idea that bodies evolve over time while the soul, or atman, continues its journey through different forms actually fits rather neatly within Hindu metaphysics. For them, evolution can be seen not just as a biological process but as a physical reflection of a deeper spiritual progression.

In modern India, acceptance of evolution varies, partly based on education, region, and exposure to Western fundamentalism. But overall, Hinduism doesn't carry the same theological friction with science as in some strains of Christianity or Islam. It doesn't need to fight science to preserve its authority. If anything, it tends to absorb new knowledge and reinterpret its stories to match what is discovered, rather than oppose it.

After reviewing the evidence for evolution and its reception across scientific and religious traditions, a deeper question remains: What does it all mean? If life is the product of natural selection, random mutation, and billions of years of trial and error, then what role do meaning, morality, or purpose play in the human story?

This is where evolution begins to stretch beyond biology and enter philosophy. Evolution doesn't offer moral prescriptions. It explains how species survive, not how they should live. It shows the mechanics of development but says nothing about justice, compassion, or purpose. This silence creates tension for people raised in traditions that teach that life is purposeful by design, that suffering serves a function, and that morality is handed down from a higher power. Evolution, in contrast, suggests that we are not the center of creation, but just one branch of an unplanned, indifferent tree of life.

That can feel hollow. "If" evolution is true, then nature doesn't care if a species thrives or goes extinct. It just operates. Lions kill. Deer flee. Bacteria mutate. Some traits get passed on. Others die with the host. The process is blind to suffering. It's not evil. It's not good. It's just indifferent. And yet, from that indifference came creatures capable of asking why. From mindless particles and selection pressure emerged human beings who write poetry, mourn their dead, tell stories, build temples, and design telescopes to stare into the origins of the universe. This is the paradox: evolution gave rise to consciousness, and consciousness turned around and asked if evolution was enough.

The challenge, then, is how to derive meaning in a world shaped by a process that doesn't inherently offer any. For some, that means rejecting the idea that evolution can be the whole story. For others, it's about finding purpose within the framework of science. Not imposed from above but created from within. Evolution shows us that cooperation, empathy, and social bonding are not just moral ideals but advantageous traits that helped our species survive. Morality didn't descend from the sky. It emerged through survival and community. That doesn't make it less real. It makes it more powerful; morality becomes something biologically wired to pursue, not just something we're told to obey.

Purpose, too, becomes something internal. If the universe has no built-in goal, then it's on us to decide what matters. For some, that may still involve God. For others, it's the pursuit of knowledge, creativity, love, or legacy. As physicist Brian Cox once said, "We are the Cosmos made conscious, and life is the means by which the universe understands itself." That's not divine prophecy. It's a recognition that evolution, by pure statistical chance, has produced beings capable of awareness. And in that awareness lies the ability to care, not just about surviving, but about living well, asking questions, and choosing what kind of world we want to build.

So, while evolution may strip away the comforting illusions of being designed with a predetermined purpose, it offers something just as profound: the freedom to define meaning in our own terms. It doesn't give the why, but the how, and from there, the why is ours to create. In a universe governed by chance and necessity, it is our consciousness, not divine design, that now holds the pen.

4

The Minds Defense

The human mind is not a neutral processor of information. It does not simply absorb facts, weigh them objectively, and adjust beliefs accordingly. Instead, it tends to filter new information through a complex web of prior experiences, emotions, social attachments, and unconscious biases. As a result, even the most unmistakable scientific evidence can be dismissed, distorted, or entirely ignored when it conflicts with deeply held beliefs. The resistance is not always rooted in ignorance or lack of education; it is often rooted in identity.

This chapter explores why belief systems, once formed, are so difficult to dislodge, even in the face of strong contradictory evidence. While previous chapters have examined the structure of belief, the power of the scientific method, and the compelling evidence for evolution, this chapter turns inward to explore how and why the brain resists change. Concepts like confirmation bias, cognitive dissonance, and the backfire effect help explain why presenting facts is often insufficient. In many cases, confronting someone with evidence that contradicts their worldview does not lead to reflection; it leads to entrenchment.

The goal here is not to shame irrationality, but to understand it. Human cognition evolved not to seek truth at all costs, but to preserve coherence, minimize threats, and maintain group cohesion. Beliefs often serve emotional and social purposes before they serve logical ones. Until these psychological functions are acknowledged, attempts to correct misinformation or challenge false beliefs will likely fall flat. Understanding how the mind resists evidence is the next step toward bridging the unknown, not by force, but by empathy and insight.

Beliefs are not simply ideas that individuals hold about the world. They are often reflections of who a person is, where they come from, and how they understand their place in a social group. When a belief becomes tied to identity, it functions less like a proposition to be tested and more like a membership badge. In these cases, challenging a belief is not merely a request to reconsider a claim; it can feel like an attack on the person.

Yale Law Professor and psychologist Dan Kahan has extensively researched this subject, particularly in science communication. Kahan coined the term "identity-protective cognition" to describe how individuals unconsciously process information in ways that preserve their group affiliations and social standing. His studies reveal that people reject facts not because they are unintelligent or uninformed, but because accepting certain information could threaten their social identity or standing within their community.

For example, Kahan's research found that political or cultural identities can distort people's ability to interpret data correctly. In one study, participants were shown the same set of numbers but came to different conclusions depending on whether the data were labeled as being about gun control or skin cream. Those who identified strongly with pro-gun or anti-gun views interpreted the same statistics differently, showing that reasoning itself can be shaped by identity cues. The more capable people were at numeracy, the more pronounced the bias became, suggesting that intelligence does not guard against motivated reasoning; it can amplify it when one's identity is on the line.

This identity-protective cognition plays a significant role in why people resist scientific claims that conflict with their worldview. For someone whose religious identity centers on a literal interpretation of scripture, accepting evolution is not just an intellectual shift; it may feel like a betrayal of family, faith, and self. Likewise, for someone whose political identity is built around skepticism of environmental regulation, accepting the scientific consensus on climate change might be interpreted as capitulating to the "other side."

Another relevant concept is belief perseverance, the psychological tendency to maintain a belief even after the evidence supporting it has been discredited. This effect is strengthened by emotional investment and social reinforcement. Even when people are presented with clear, disconfirming evidence, they often rationalize or dismiss it to preserve internal consistency and avoid the discomfort of cognitive dissonance. This is especially true when beliefs are held publicly or within tight-knit communities where deviation comes with social cost. Understanding belief as a component of identity changes how we approach disagreement. Simply presenting facts is often ineffective, not because the facts are wrong, but because the psychological cost of changing one's mind can be too high. This insight is critical for anyone bridging the gap between science and belief. If new information is perceived as a threat to selfhood or social belonging, it will be rejected, not on its logical merits, but for self-preservation.

To make progress, science communication and education must go beyond the transfer of information. They must account for the social and emotional architecture of belief. Respecting identity while inviting curiosity is far more effective than confrontation. People rarely change their minds when they feel attacked, but they sometimes reconsider when they feel safe, seen, and understood.

Even when people genuinely strive to think clearly, their minds are shaped by built-in shortcuts that affect how they interpret information. These shortcuts, known as cognitive biases, evolved to help humans make fast decisions in uncertain or dangerous situations. While they can be helpful in everyday life, they often work against rational thinking, especially when someone is confronted with evidence that challenges their core beliefs.

One of the most well-known of these patterns is confirmation bias. This bias leads people to notice, seek out, and remember information that supports what they already believe, while ignoring or minimizing anything that contradicts it. For example, someone skeptical of evolution may focus on fringe claims or out-of-context quotes that appear to discredit the theory, even while dismissing the vast amount of peer-reviewed research that supports it. In today's digital environment, this tendency is often reinforced by social media platforms that show users more of the content they already agree with, further insulating them from alternative viewpoints.

A closely related concept is motivated reasoning. While confirmation bias influences what information people notice, motivated reasoning shapes how they interpret that information. Instead of asking whether something is true, the brain often asks whether it feels right or supports an existing worldview. This can lead people to use their reasoning skills not to explore ideas openly, but to defend the ones they are already invested in. In many cases, those with higher levels of education or intelligence are even more skilled at rationalizing incorrect beliefs because they have more tools to make their arguments sound convincing.

Sometimes, when a belief is strongly tied to identity or emotion, presenting factual corrections can make matters worse. This is where the backfire effect comes into play. In these cases, direct attempts to correct misinformation can actually strengthen a person's original belief. Although the backfire effect may not occur in every situation, it highlights a more profound truth: challenging someone's worldview often feels threatening. When people feel pressured or exposed, their natural response is to resist, not reflect. Together, these biases reveal a simple but uncomfortable fact: facts alone are rarely enough to change minds. The brain tends to protect beliefs that offer a sense of stability, belonging, or identity. It prefers coherence over contradiction, and comfort over uncertainty. What once may have helped humans survive in close-knit tribes now makes it difficult to process complex, unfamiliar, or uncomfortable truths.

Understanding these cognitive patterns is essential for anyone who wants to foster honest dialogue. Education that teaches people to recognize these biases in themselves (rather than just spotting them in others) can build the foundation for deeper thinking. Awareness, humility, and curiosity are not just intellectual virtues; they are necessary tools for overcoming the mental habits that keep people locked into false certainty.

Although humans often think of themselves as rational beings, the truth is that emotions play a far greater role in shaping beliefs than most people realize. Logic and evidence may influence our thinking, but rarely drive it entirely. In many cases, people accept or reject ideas not because of the strength of the argument, but because of how those ideas make them feel.

Emotions act as an internal compass, shaping what feels true long before the conscious mind begins to reason through the details. When a scientific claim aligns with someone's values or brings a sense of comfort, it is easier to accept. But it can trigger feelings of fear, anger, or confusion when it threatens something important (like a moral conviction, a sense of identity, or a belief about the world). These reactions are important, and they often override calm, rational thought.

Neuroscience supports this understanding. The brain processes emotional information faster than logical information. The limbic system, which governs emotional responses, reacts almost instantly to perceived threats. The rational part of the brain, the prefrontal cortex, takes longer to catch up. This means that by the time a person begins to consider evidence, they may already be influenced by how the evidence makes them feel. If the emotional response is strong enough, no amount of reasoning may be able to undo it. This is why debates about evolution, climate change, or vaccines often feel more like emotional battles than intellectual discussions. When someone feels personally attacked or morally judged, they are unlikely to reconsider their views, no matter how carefully the evidence is presented. The resistance is not always about the facts themselves. It is about the emotional meaning attached to those facts. Understanding this emotional dimension helps explain why persuasion often fails when it relies only on logic. People are more likely to open their minds when they feel safe, respected, and understood. A belief that is emotionally held cannot be dislodged through reason alone. It requires empathy, patience, and often a willingness to listen rather than to argue.

In this way, the path to truth is not just intellectual. It is emotional and relational. Before someone can reconsider a belief, they must feel that doing so will not cost them their dignity, place in a community, or sense of meaning. Logic may light the way, but emotion determines whether the journey even begins.

Changing a deeply held belief is rarely just an intellectual decision. It often comes with real social consequences. For many people, beliefs are not only private conclusions but public commitments that connect them to family, culture, religion, or political communities. Letting go of those beliefs, even in the face of strong evidence, can mean risking relationships, losing status, or becoming isolated from the people and traditions they hold dear.

This social dimension of belief is one of the strongest reasons why facts alone are often not enough to change minds. When a belief serves as a marker of belonging, questioning it can create emotional and interpersonal tension. For example, a student raised in a religious household may understand the science of evolution but hesitate to accept it fully, knowing that doing so might lead to conflict at home or even rejection from their community. The decision to believe or disbelieve becomes less about truth and more about survival within a social structure.

Sociologists and psychologists have documented how communities often reinforce belief systems through shared rituals, language, and moral boundaries. These structures create strong incentives to conform and substantial penalties for deviation. In tightly knit groups, changing one's belief can feel like a betrayal—not just of ideas but of people. This is especially true in environments where group identity is tied to certainty and where doubt is viewed as weakness or disloyalty.

Stories of individuals who leave political movements, religious traditions, or ideological bubbles often reveal a long process filled with fear, grief, and loneliness. Some describe the pain of losing friends or being cut off from family. Others speak of the struggle to rebuild a worldview without the scaffolding they once relied on. Even when the new belief feels more truthful, the cost of change can be emotionally overwhelming. A personal example of this is one of my fathers. He was a pastor for 7 years before he realigned his beliefs to question the legitimacy of Hell. He then wrote a book called *What the Hell,* which essentially reads into the scriptures that teach about this subject and where this idea of Hell came from. It was a book rooted in the honest pursuit of truth. After he spoke up about his beliefs on the subject, he was fired from the church where he worked. Recognizing the social cost of belief change helps explain why some people cling to ideas that may seem irrational from the outside. What looks like stubbornness is often a form of self-protection. It is not just the belief at stake—it is a sense of home, connection, and identity.

Any effort to encourage open-mindedness must take this into account. Creating environments where people can question ideas without fear of rejection is essential. Change becomes possible when individuals feel that their dignity, belonging, and relationships will not be destroyed in the process. Before someone can let go of an old belief, they need to know they will not fall alone.

If belief is tied to identity and the mind is shaped by emotion, bias, and social influence, then a key step toward clearer thinking is recognizing the limits of one's own certainty. This mindset is known as intellectual humility—the willingness to accept that one's knowledge is incomplete, that assumptions can be wrong, and that truth is often more complex than it first appears.

Intellectual humility is not the same as self-doubt or indecision. It does not mean that every belief must be constantly questioned or that people should avoid forming firm conclusions. Instead, it means holding convictions lightly enough to allow for correction. It means listening not just to respond, but to understand. It is the recognition that being wrong is not a failure, but part of the learning process.

Psychological research has increasingly shown that intellectual humility plays a critical role in how individuals interact with evidence, opposing viewpoints, and their learning. A 2020 study by Krumrei-Mancuso and colleagues found that individuals who score high in intellectual humility tend to be more receptive to counter-attitudinal information, more likely to revise inaccurate beliefs, and better able to evaluate arguments on their merits rather than on personal alignment. They are also less likely to rely on cognitive distortions such as stereotyping or overgeneralization. This makes them more flexible thinkers and, over time, more effective learners.

These findings suggest that people who demonstrate intellectual humility do not base their identity on being right. Instead, they build an identity around curiosity, growth, and a willingness to honestly self-examine. They are more likely to say "I don't know" when they lack information and are more willing to listen carefully to views they initially disagree with.

Fostering this mindset requires more than just teaching critical thinking in schools. It requires teachers, leaders, and role models to model humility. It also depends on the presence of safe environments (both in classrooms and in public discourse) where disagreement is not punished, questions are not dismissed, and being wrong is treated as a necessary part of growth.

Humility can seem out of place in a fast-paced world that often rewards performance and loud opinions. Yet it remains essential for bridging belief and evidence. Intellectual humility allows people to maintain conviction while still being open to change. Growth does not require abandoning all beliefs, only the willingness to revise them when the evidence calls for it. The strongest thinkers are not those who cling to fixed ideas, but those who remain willing to be changed by what they learn.

The desire to persuade others is often driven by a belief that truth is self-evident. If the facts are strong enough and the logic is clear, people should change their minds. But human beings are not logic machines. They are meaning-makers. What they accept as truth is rarely determined by data alone. It is filtered through the deeper architecture of identity, emotion, community, memory, and fear. To persuade someone without first understanding that architecture is to speak to the surface of the mind while the roots remain untouched.

This chapter has explored why belief can be so resistant to evidence. It is not always because of ignorance or willful denial. Often, the resistance is rooted in self-preservation. Beliefs, especially core ones, help people make sense of the world. They offer security in uncertainty, coherence in chaos, and belonging in isolation. To question a belief is not simply to entertain a new idea. It is to open a door that may not lead anywhere safe.

That is why understanding must come before persuasion. Before asking someone to change, one must ask what that change would cost them. Would it mean losing their community? Their moral compass? Their sense of who they are? These are not small sacrifices and cannot be addressed with facts alone. To truly engage with belief, one must meet it not with confrontation but compassion, not with superiority, but with curiosity.

Philosopher Søren Kierkegaard once wrote that all true help begins with humility—the humility to locate the other person where they are and meet them there. This is as true in science communication as in any human interaction. One cannot lift someone up by shouting from above. One must descend into their perspective, understand it on its own terms, and only then offer a way forward.

There is also a moral dimension to persuasion. The impulse to correct others often hides a deeper desire to correct oneself. But if the goal is not simply to win an argument, but to invite someone into deeper understanding, then the act of persuasion must become an act of care. It must make room for uncertainty and allow space for gradual change. It must respect the person's dignity, even when challenging their ideas.

In this light, intellectual humility is not just a cognitive tool. It becomes an ethical stance. It acknowledges that no one has the full picture, and that understanding is constantly unfolding. Persuasion rooted in this humility does not demand submission. It invites reflection. It does not tear down identity. It encourages it to expand. Science, when it is healthy, reflects this process. It thrives not by holding firm to dogma but by constantly questioning, revising, and refining its view of reality. This is a model not only for knowledge, but for conversation. Those who wish to bridge the divide between belief and evidence must learn to speak in the same spirit, not as enforcers of truth but fellow seekers.

Ultimately, progress is not marked by how many minds are changed in a single debate. It is measured by the quiet moments when a person feels safe enough to say, "Maybe I was wrong." Or even better, "I want to understand more." Those moments are not loud. They are not easy to measure. But they are where transformation begins. And it is there, in the quiet space between certainty and curiosity, that the real work of bridging the unknown takes place.

5

The Discipline of Truth

Truth doesn't care how something feels. It isn't measured by certainty or comfort. It doesn't adjust itself to match tradition or emotional need. And yet, most people never learn how to distinguish between what's true and what's simply convincing.

That's not because they're unintelligent — they've never been taught how to know.

We grow up learning what to believe, not how to evaluate beliefs. We're taught rules, stories, and slogans. But rarely are we taught the difference between evidence and opinion, or why being convinced doesn't always mean being correct. In a world that's drowning in information, this missing skill is dangerous.

Knowing what's true—or at least, what's *most likely* true—requires more than intuition. It requires tools. Science isn't just a collection of facts. It's a method. A process designed to eliminate bias, challenge assumptions, and refine our understanding through testing and repetition. At its core, science is a way of asking: *If I'm wrong, how would I know?*

Most belief systems don't ask that question. They protect themselves from it. But truth isn't threatened by scrutiny. Only illusion is.

Critical thinking, skepticism, falsifiability — these are not just intellectual exercises. They are how we protect ourselves from being fooled. They are how we keep our convictions honest. They don't guarantee we'll always be right, but they dramatically reduce the chances of living in confident error.

The brain is built to make quick judgments. It prefers simplicity, coherence, and emotional resolution. But truth often resists those things. It's messy. It evolves. It asks for patience, not instant answers. That's why real knowledge is hard and so few people are trained to pursue it.

Truth-seeking isn't about cynicism. It's about discipline. It's about holding our beliefs to the same standard we would expect of others. It means asking not just *"Do I believe this?"* but *"Should I?"* And it means walking away from ideas that don't hold up under pressure — even if they once felt like home.

One of the most critical tools in the pursuit of truth is falsifiability — the idea that a claim must be testable and potentially disprovable. This concept, championed by philosopher Karl Popper, helps separate science from pseudoscience. If a belief can't be tested, if it can't be proven wrong even in theory, then it doesn't belong in the realm of knowledge. It's not that it's false — it's that it's unfalsifiable. That makes it immune to correction.

Beliefs that can't be challenged aren't strong — they're brittle. They don't grow, they don't adapt, and they don't improve with time. They persist.

Another challenge in knowing what's true is our own confirmation bias — the tendency to seek out and favor information that supports what we already believe. This bias isn't a personal flaw. It's part of how the brain works. We filter reality through expectations. We remember things that fit our views and ignore those that don't. We interpret neutral data in a way that confirms our instincts. Without awareness of this bias, we reinforce our assumptions, no matter how shaky they are.

This is why asking questions, especially uncomfortable ones, is crucial. It's not about doubting everything. It's about creating a system where doubt has a place. It's about ensuring our beliefs are shaped by reality, not vice versa.

Cognitive ease also plays a role. Ideas that are familiar or fluently worded feel more true. This has nothing to do with accuracy. A false claim repeated often enough starts to feel real simply because the brain prefers ease over effort. This is one reason propaganda works — it feels smooth and accurate.

The antidote to these mental traps isn't constant suspicion. It's awareness. It's knowing how the mind tricks itself so we can build habits that resist those tricks. Seeking truth means slowing down. It means testing ideas, examining sources, and being willing to say, *"I was wrong."*

But none of these tools matter if they're only applied to other people's beliefs. Real intellectual honesty starts with our own. It asks, *"Would I believe this if I hadn't grown up around it?"* *"Would I accept this argument if it came from someone I disagreed with?"* These aren't easy questions, but they matter.

Belief doesn't start with a conscious choice. It begins with exposure.

Before we ever ask, "Is this true?", we are immersed in a reality shaped by the people around us. Parents, teachers, preachers, and peers don't usually present their beliefs as *beliefs*. They present them as facts, norms, and the way the world simply is.

And so, we absorb. We internalize. Before we can critically examine a claim, we've already begun living inside it.

This is the machinery of indoctrination — not always as a sinister force, but as a structural flaw in how humans are raised. It's the difference between being told *what* to think and being taught *how* to think. Most people are trained for acceptance, not inquiry. The child who questions too much is called difficult. The adult who challenges the status quo is called dangerous. But those labels don't reflect a problem with the questionnaire — they reflect a system that thrives on unexamined loyalty.

The institutions that shape us—religious, cultural, political, even educational—often have more interest in stability than in truth. Stability requires cohesion, which requires shared beliefs. Shared beliefs are easiest to maintain when instilled early and protected from scrutiny.

But this kind of unity comes at a cost: the erosion of intellectual autonomy.

A person taught to believe without evidence is being trained in obedience, not wisdom. They may memorize facts, recite doctrines, and follow rules, but remain vulnerable to manipulation because they lack the tools to question the source.

A truly educated person is dangerous to dogma. They don't just accept claims, they dissect them. They don't just accumulate knowledge, they interrogate it. And that's why critical thinking is so rare: not because it's hard, but because it's subversive.

We must reverse the pipeline if we want a society that values truth over comfort. Instead of raising children to inherit belief systems, we must raise them to evaluate them. Instead of teaching *what* to believe, we must teach *why* belief matters — and how easily it can go wrong.

Imagine if we taught skepticism as early as we taught spelling. Suppose every child learned the difference between correlation and causation, between anecdote and data, between assertion and argument. Imagine if "How do you know?" was treated not as defiance, but as virtue.

Without that shift or cultural commitment to cognitive self-defense, we remain prey to those who would rather have followers than thinkers.

Belief is rarely just an idea. It's often a costume—one we've worn so long that it starts to feel like skin.

That's why it hurts to question it. Not just intellectually, but emotionally. Questioning a core belief doesn't feel like changing a thought; it feels like amputating a limb. The discomfort isn't just cognitive dissonance. It's existential dissonance.

We are social creatures. We're built for belonging. So when belief becomes the ticket to community — to love, respect, and safety — abandoning that belief comes with a price. It might mean alienation. Estrangement. Even exile. And this is precisely why so many people cling to beliefs they no longer intellectually accept: the social cost of honesty feels greater than the personal cost of self- deception.

This is especially true in tight-knit communities, where the boundary between belief and identity is blurred. In such spaces, you don't just *believe* in a religion — you *are* that religion. You don't just support a political party — you *are* that party. And the moment you begin to question, you're not just doubting an idea — you're betraying a tribe.

This makes the pursuit of truth a kind of rebellion—not just against misinformation but against the psychological architecture of identity itself.

The tragedy is that we are taught to equate integrity with consistency. We're told that "standing by your beliefs" signifies character. But that only makes sense if your beliefs are worthy of being stood by. Absolute integrity isn't about rigidity — it's about responsiveness. It's about being willing to change direction when the evidence leads elsewhere. It's about recognizing that *who we are* is not diminished by *what we revise*.

There's also a strange irony here: the more fragile a belief is, the more sacred it tends to become. The more emotionally invested we are in it, the less we allow ourselves to question it, and the more aggressively we defend it from others. But strength isn't the absence of scrutiny. It's the ability to survive it.

Beliefs tied too closely to identity become un-updatable. And anything un-updatable is unresponsive to reality. That's not stability — that's intellectual paralysis.

We must learn to decouple who we are from what we believe. We should hold our ideas in open hands, not clenched fists. To measure our convictions not by how deeply we feel them, but by how well they stand up to challenge. That's the difference between growth and stagnation. Between learning and clinging. Between a mind that evolves and a mind that ossifies.

Earlier in this book, I wrote about the emotional gravity of certainty — how belief offers a kind of psychological shelter. But when belief fuses with identity, the shelter becomes a cage.

People don't cling to false ideas because they're irrational. They cling because the concept is tied to who they think they are. And walking away from it would feel like erasing part of themselves, or losing the community that gave that identity meaning in the first place.

When belief is tied to belonging, truth becomes secondary.

This is why most arguments fail. They confront the content of the belief without acknowledging the cost of abandoning it. They provide better facts but ignore the social trauma of letting go. Changing your mind, in this context, means risking exile from your church, your family, your culture, from the people who raised you.

Chapter 4 explored how the mind resists contradiction — how we filter, twist, and reframe reality to preserve internal consistency. But that reflex intensifies when the belief in question is part of your identity. At that point, it's not about being correct. It's about staying whole.

A climate change denier doesn't necessarily reject the data. They reject what it would mean to admit it — that they'd have to change, that their tribe might abandon them, that they might have been wrong for a long time. The human mind, wired for social cohesion, will often distort facts to avoid that pain.

This is why truth-seeking is not a purely intellectual act. It's emotional, relational, and asks us to give up comfort, certainty, and sometimes community. And that's not easy, but it is necessary.

Because beliefs tied too tightly to identity become brittle. They can't evolve. They can't improve. They can only persist, defended not by evidence, but by fear.

By now, it should be clear that truth isn't something we stumble into. It's something we must build toward — deliberately, patiently, and often uncomfortably.

In Chapter 2, I discussed how belief can be a psychological resting place —certainty soothes the anxious mind. And in Chapter 4, I explored how the brain resists correction, even when presented with contradictory evidence. Those chapters show that our instincts often mislead us, not because we are broken, but because we evolved to prioritize coherence, belonging, and emotional resolution over factual precision. The brain wants stories that feel right, not necessarily ones that *are* right. But once we recognize these tendencies, we gain the power to resist them. And that resistance begins with tools.

Truth-seeking is not an innate trait. It's a learned discipline. It takes more than good intentions to avoid self-deception — it takes structure. Habits. A method. These are not abstract virtues, but concrete practices designed to catch our errors before they catch us. They don't guarantee absolute certainty. But they give us something better: a process we can trust, even when we can't fully trust ourselves.

One of the most powerful tools (as mentioned earlier) is falsifiability — the idea that a belief must be testable and contain the possibility of being proven wrong within itself. A claim that cannot be disproven isn't strong — it's sterile. Unlike many belief systems, science draws its strength not from being unchallengeable, but from being *constantly* challenged. That vulnerability is precisely what makes it trustworthy. It can correct itself. It evolves.

Another tool is Occam's Razor — the principle that, all else being equal, the simplest explanation is usually the best starting point. It doesn't mean the most straightforward answer is always correct. But if your belief relies on layers of speculation, conspiracy, or exception-making to stay intact, it's worth asking whether it's being propped up by narrative rather than necessity.

Closely tied to this is the Principle of Charity — the discipline of assuming that those we disagree with are arguing in good faith. When we steelman someone's position and try to understand their argument at its strongest rather than its weakest, we sharpen our own thinking. We learn to listen, not just react. We trade reflex for reflection.

Cognitive reflection is also vital. Our minds are built for speed, not depth. The first conclusion that pops into our heads often feels the truest, but that's not because it *is* true. It's because it's familiar, emotionally resonant, or socially convenient. Slowing down and asking, "Why does this feel right?" is a small act of rebellion against our biases.

And finally, there is skepticism — not the cynical kind that dismisses everything, but the disciplined kind that asks for good reasons before granting belief. Real skepticism treats belief not as a default, but as a responsibility. It's not about doubting *everything* — it's about refusing to believe without evidence.

When practiced consistently, these tools form a kind of intellectual immune system. They don't make you immune to error, but make you far more likely to detect it early. They protect not just what you think, but *how* you think.

And like any immune system, these tools are only practical if applied internally first. It's easy to point out bias in others. It's much harder — and infinitely more important — to detect it in ourselves. As I've said before, absolute intellectual honesty begins with the question, "Would I believe this if it weren't mine?"

That question is the dividing line between belief as comfort and belief as courage, between a worldview that evolves and one that merely endures, between a mind that protects its pride and one that protects its integrity.

The pursuit of truth is not a path paved with reassurance. It's a path of friction that asks us to question the things that once comforted us. It demands more than intellect. It demands courage. To see clearly, we must often unsee what we were taught. To know honestly, we must first admit how easily we can be fooled.

This chapter has explored the architecture of truth-seeking, not as an abstract philosophical exercise, but as a daily discipline. We've seen how our minds crave coherence over clarity, how belief systems shield themselves from scrutiny, and how identity can turn ideas into sacred territory. But we've also seen that awareness is power. That tools like falsifiability, skepticism, and reflection don't just make us better thinkers — they make us freer ones.

The greatest danger in belief isn't that it might be wrong. It's that we might never know. When conviction is allowed to outrun evidence, emotion replaces evaluation, and comfort becomes the standard for truth, we don't just risk being mistaken. We risk being uncorrectable.

And that's the deeper cost of abandoning the pursuit of truth: not just that we get things wrong, but that we build lives, policies, and identities on those wrong things. What we believe shapes what we value. And what we value determines how we treat each other. This is why truth matters.

Not just in science. Not just in politics. But in ethics. In community. In how we love, how we choose, and how we live. If we are willing to hold ourselves to the same standard we demand of others — if we are eager to walk away from beautiful lies and face uncomfortable realities — then the pursuit of truth doesn't just make us smarter. It will make us more human.

In the next chapter, we will ask what happens after the illusions disappear. If we no longer tether morality to mythology, what takes its place? Can ethics survive without certainty, and can meaning exist without belief?

The search continues — not for what we were told to believe, but for what remains when belief is no longer enough.

6

The Human Invention of Goodness

One of the most common assumptions about religion is that it holds a monopoly on morality. Remove God, we're told, and the floor falls out — anything becomes permissible. If there's no one watching or judging, what's stopping us from doing whatever we want? For many, the idea of a godless world doesn't just feel intellectually barren. It feels ethically unanchored. The absence of divine authority is imagined as a moral vacuum — a place where nihilism, selfishness, and chaos rush in.

However, this view misunderstands both morality and human nature.

It assumes that people are moral only because they fear punishment or crave reward. That our compassion is conditional, our empathy transactional, and our conscience outsourced to scripture. It assumes that without a cosmic referee, we'd all become monsters. And yet, there is no evidence for this. Secular societies consistently show lower rates of violent crime, higher levels of social trust, and greater investment in public welfare than their more religious counterparts. If morality were impossible without belief, these data wouldn't exist.

More importantly, it assumes that ethics must be handed down, not worked out.

But what if morality isn't a divine decree? What if it's a human invention — not in the sense of being fake or arbitrary, but in the sense of being collaborative, adaptive, and deeply real? What if the same faculties that help us discover what's true can also help us decide what's good?

The last chapter explored how truth-seeking requires discipline — a toolkit of reflection, skepticism, and self-awareness. Morality, it turns out, demands the same. If belief can be evaluated, so can values. If convictions can be tested for coherence and consequence, then ethics, like knowledge, becomes not a handed-down command, but a living process — one built from the ground up, not the sky down.

This chapter is about that process. It's about what happens when we untether morality from mythology — and discover that it doesn't fall apart. It gets stronger.

For all its influence, religious morality is not the ethical stronghold it's often made out to be. When scrutinized, it reveals a host of problems, not just in its historical consequences, but in its very foundations. It is often less a coherent moral system and more a series of inherited taboos, ancient customs, and divine decrees that resist questioning precisely because they come from authority.

At the core of most religious ethics lies the idea of *divine command* — the belief that something is good because God says so. But this logic collapses under the slightest philosophical pressure. As raised in Plato's *Euthyphro*, the dilemma is simple: Is something good because God commands it, or does God command it because it is good? If the former, then morality is arbitrary — anything God decrees, even cruelty, becomes "good" by fiat. If the latter, then goodness exists independently of God, and divine command is unnecessary. Either way, religious morality loses its foundation.

Worse, much of what we find in scripture is morally indefensible by modern standards. The Bible condones slavery. The Qur'an allows for polygamy and corporal punishment. The Torah outlines rituals for stoning adulterers and executing homosexuals. These aren't metaphorical passages. Their moral laws are presented as divinely sanctioned. To dismiss them today as "cultural" or "contextual" is to admit that we have already begun judging scripture by a higher moral standard — one that evolves and comes from elsewhere.

And that's the point: moral progress doesn't come from obedience. It comes from disobedience. From pushing back. From questioning what we were told and daring to ask whether it still holds. Every significant moral advance — from the abolition of slavery to women's rights to LGBTQ+ equality — was opposed by religious authorities before it was accepted. These victories didn't arise because people followed holy books. They occurred because people challenged them.

Religious morality also depends heavily on consequences that lie beyond this life. Do good, and you'll be rewarded in heaven. Do evil, and you'll suffer in hell. But a morality based on eternal reward or punishment isn't morality — it's coercion. It confuses obedience with goodness. It teaches people to act not out of empathy or integrity, but out of fear. Strip away the afterlife, and the entire framework loses its leverage.

But morality shouldn't need leverage. If compassion requires the threat of damnation, it isn't compassion. If kindness must be purchased with paradise, it's not kindness — it's bargaining.

This isn't to say that religious people cannot be good. Clearly, they can. But they aren't good *because* of religion. They're good in spite of it — or because their moral intuitions, their empathy, their social context, or their upbringing emphasized decency more than dogma. The problem isn't that religion can't contain good values. The problem is that it anchors those values to claims that cannot be questioned.

And anything that cannot be questioned cannot improve.

Real morality must be dynamic. It must evolve in response to suffering, evidence, and understanding. It must be sensitive to context and open to revision. But religious morality, by design, resists change. It sanctifies the past and freezes ethical thought in time. That might offer stability, but it comes at the cost of progress.

If morality is going to matter — if it's going to protect people, uplift society, and adapt to a changing world — then it must be able to grow. And for that to happen, it must be rooted not in revelation but reason.

If morality doesn't come from divine command, where does it come from? The answer isn't mysterious. It's written in our biology, evolution, and shared experience as social animals. We didn't invent morality from thin air — we inherited the instincts for it. Long before the first religious text was carved into stone, our ancestors had already negotiated fairness, reciprocity, and cooperation, not because of commandments, but because of survival.

Empathy is not a spiritual gift. It's a neurological function. Mirror neurons fire when we see someone else in pain, triggering the same regions in our brain that would activate if we were hurting ourselves. This is why a child winces when another falls, or why we flinch at on-screen violence. Compassion isn't learned from holy books. It emerges from a brain wired to care because caring helped us thrive.

In evolutionary terms, moral behavior was adaptive. Humans are uniquely dependent on cooperation. We don't survive alone—we survive in groups. Groups that punished selfishness, encouraged fairness, and protected the vulnerable were more likely to endure. These behaviors became internalized. We developed instincts for justice and revulsion toward cruelty. What we call "conscience" isn't a divine whisper. It's a survival mechanism, honed over thousands of generations.

This doesn't make morality less meaningful. If anything, it makes it more remarkable, because it's ours. It belongs not to gods, but to the species. It emerges not from heaven, but from the messy, tangible needs of real creatures trying to coexist.

Psychologist Jonathan Haidt has shown that moral intuitions cluster around core principles — care, fairness, loyalty, authority, sanctity, and liberty. These aren't commandments etched into stone; they're evolved dimensions of moral concern that different cultures emphasize differently. But across time and place, the concern for harm and well-being — the impulse to reduce suffering and increase flourishing — remains universal.

Even infants show a rudimentary sense of fairness. In controlled experiments, babies as young as six months prefer puppets who help others over those who hinder them. They show surprise or distress when unfair distributions occur. This isn't theology. It's biology. It's evidence that moral intuitions precede religious instruction.

None of this is to say that humans are inherently good. We're not. We're capable of extraordinary cruelty. But our capacity for morality—empathy, justice, and compassion—doesn't come from fear of divine punishment. It comes from our nature as social beings. And like all biological capacities, it can be cultivated or suppressed depending on the environment.

Religion is just organized and institutionalized, and it is often claimed to have ownership of it. However, the ethical instincts that keep us from hurting one another existed long before religion arrived, and they remain just as powerful when unshackled from mythology. They may become *more* powerful because they're no longer constrained by dogma. They're free to evolve, expand, and respond to new forms of harm and understandings of justice.

Secular ethics doesn't reduce morality to mere instinct. It refines it. It asks: What works? What promotes well-being? What minimizes harm? It also allows for correction when the answers change. In the end, that may be the most ethical thing of all — not believing that we've already arrived at truth, but staying open to the possibility that we can get closer.

If morality doesn't come from divine command, and if our evolutionary wiring gives us only the starting material, then ethics becomes something we must consciously construct. That may sound unstable to those used to eternal commandments — but in reality, it's precisely what makes secular morality so adaptable. It can evolve. It can be refined. And most importantly, it can be tested.

A moral system that relies on obedience is brittle. A moral system that relies on outcomes is responsive.

This is where frameworks like utilitarianism come in — not as perfect answers, but as examples of morality when grounded in evidence and consequence rather than revelation. At its core, utilitarian ethics is simple: the best action is the one that produces the greatest overall good or reduces the most significant amount of harm. It doesn't ask what God commands. It asks what helps people flourish. What reduces suffering? What makes life better, not in theory, but in practice?

Critics often paint utilitarianism as cold, calculating, or overly simplistic. And yes, it can be misapplied — like any tool. But at its best, it offers something religion rarely can: a framework that adjusts based on new data. If we discover, for instance, that a policy we thought was good increases long-term harm, a consequence-based ethic allows us to correct course. It doesn't require a prophet. It requires honesty.

Another pillar of secular ethics is humanism — the idea that moral worth is grounded not in divine image but shared humanity. Humanism emphasizes dignity, autonomy, and compassion as values in themselves. It does not promise eternal reward. It promises the chance to live a meaningful life here and now, with a responsibility to others trying to do the same. In a world without divine supervision, morality doesn't disappear — it becomes more urgent. We are each other's only stewards.

A modern example of this is effective altruism, a movement grounded in both heart and reason. Its goal isn't just to *do* good, but to do the *most* good — to maximize impact by applying data, critical thinking, and cost-benefit analysis to charitable giving and social action. It asks difficult questions, like: How many lives does this actually save? Could the same money prevent more suffering elsewhere? It challenges the idea that good intentions are enough and insists that compassion be paired with clarity.

These approaches may differ in emphasis, but they share a fundamental trait: they treat morality as a human endeavor, not a script to follow, not a project to build. And that project demands tools: reason, evidence, empathy, and a commitment to results.

Even our most abstract moral dilemmas — the trolley problem, for example — force us to weigh outcomes, intentions, and human costs. These aren't just thought experiments. They're a reflection of how real-life ethics work when we don't have a list of divine instructions to defer to. In a complex world, ethical questions rarely come with clean answers. That's not a failure of secular morality. It's its strength. It's the recognition that ethical clarity often comes not from certainty but struggle.

In religious frameworks, moral laws are static and handed down from outside time. However, secular ethics are dynamic, forged from human experience, tested in the real world, and always subject to revision.

And that's the difference. Religion offers pre-written answers, while secular ethics offers the courage to keep asking better questions.

One of the most dangerous ideas in moral philosophy and religion is the belief that certainty equals righteousness. That if a rule has divine backing, it must be followed without question. That if a text says it's good, then it is good, regardless of consequence, context, or harm.

But certainty, in ethics, is often a liability.

History is littered with atrocities committed in the name of moral certainty. Crusades. Witch hunts. Honor killings. The Inquisition. The belief that one *knows* what is good, not thinks, not hopes, not reasons, but *knows*, is precisely what allows people to justify cruelty as virtue. When a moral code is seen as sacred and infallible, it becomes unchallengeable. And when it can't be challenged, it can't be improved.

Secular morality, by contrast, makes no such claim to perfection. It does not present itself as a final answer. It doesn't promise absolute certainty. Instead, it offers flexibility — the ability to grow, adjust, and revise. And that humility is not a weakness. It is a safeguard.

Moral progress depends on our capacity to doubt. The abolition of slavery, the expansion of women's rights, and the recognition of LGBTQ+ dignity did not happen because people followed existing moral systems. They happened because people questioned them, saw suffering where others saw tradition, and trusted empathy over obedience.

This is the paradox of moral progress: it comes not from those who clung to the answers but from those who were willing to admit they might be wrong.

Uncertainty opens the door to improvement. It keeps us listening. It forces us to remain curious, test our assumptions, and confront uncomfortable truths about ourselves and the systems we've inherited. In doing so, it builds a morality that is alive, not fossilized.

Religious moral systems often equate uncertainty with moral decay. They warn of "relativism" — the fear that without absolute standards, anything goes. But that's a false dichotomy. There is a vast difference between moral relativism and moral humility. One shrugs and says, "There is no truth." The other leans in and asks, "Are we closer yet?"

And we are closer. We've built international human rights doctrines. We've outlawed torture. We've raised awareness of systemic injustice. We've made progress not because we were certain, but because we were willing to revise what we thought was right.

That is the strength of a secular ethic. It doesn't need to be perfect to be powerful. It doesn't need to be eternal to be enduring. It only needs to be honest about what we know, what we don't, and what we can do better.

In a world where answers are easy to come by and hard to verify, the ability to say "I don't know" — and mean it — is not just intellectual integrity. It's moral courage.

If morality no longer flows from divine authority, and if certainty is replaced by moral humility, the next question becomes existential: *Then what do we live for?*
Without commandments, rituals, or cosmic narratives, does anything still matter?

This is the fear that haunts many who leave religion—the idea that meaning is tethered to belief and that without it, we're just drifting. In the absence of an ultimate purpose, life becomes hollow, directionless, or even absurd.

But that fear, like many fears rooted in belief, is an illusion. Purpose doesn't vanish when belief does. It changes direction. It stops flowing from the top down and begins to emerge from the inside out.

The truth is, meaning doesn't require myth. It requires engagement. We don't need a god to tell us what matters. We need the courage to decide that it matters anyway — even if the universe doesn't care, even if no cosmic ledger is keeping score. Love still matters. Kindness still matters. Beauty, joy, truth, justice — all of it still matters, not because it was ordained, but because *we* are here to experience it. Because it matters to *us*.

Purpose, in this view, becomes something we *build*, not *inherit*. And that is not a loss. It is a liberation.

The same impulse that once built temples can now create communities. The same psychological wiring that once served doctrine can now serve well-being. We still gather, tell stories, grieve, celebrate, and reflect. But the stories are ours. The rituals are chosen. The frameworks are not fixed—they evolve with us.

Secular purpose is not synthetic. It's self-aware. It knows it was crafted, not delivered — and that makes it more adaptable, not less. Whether raising children, creating art, advancing justice, or simply living with integrity, the values that drive us forward don't evaporate without religion. They often become clearer, because they're no longer obscured by divine command or fear of eternal punishment. They stand on their own — or they don't stand at all.

And that's a good thing.

It forces us to ask more profound questions. Not "What was I told to do?" but "What kind of world do I want to help create?" Not "What will happen to me after I die?" but "What kind of life will I leave behind?" These are the questions of a mature ethic. They require thought, effort, and sometimes grief —

but they lead to a morality that isn't just obeyed, it's owned.

Across the world, secular communities are already doing this work — designing ethical education programs, organizing mutual aid networks, and creating new ceremonies for birth, marriage, and death. They prove you don't need supernatural beliefs to experience reverence, solidarity, or belonging. You need intention. You need each other.

And in many ways, this kind of purpose is more honest. It doesn't claim to know the unknowable. It doesn't offer guarantees. It offers responsibility. It says: This world is uncertain. These lives are brief. But while we're here, let's try to make something meaningful together.

The idea that morality must be handed down is one of human history's oldest and most persistent illusions. For centuries, ethical authority was tied to sacred texts, priesthoods, and the fear of divine judgment. But what if those structures were never the source of goodness, only its packaging?

What we've explored in this chapter is not the dismantling of morality, but its liberation.

We've seen that our sense of right and wrong predates scripture, that empathy is not supernatural but neurological, that fairness evolved because it helped us survive, and that compassion endures because it makes us human. We've seen that ethics, when untethered from dogma, doesn't collapse. It adapts, it learns, and it grows stronger because it allows for correction.

A secular ethic does not offer all the answers — and that's its greatest strength. It does not pretend to speak for the universe. It speaks for us. For this moment, this planet, these lives. It is not anchored in fear or reward, but in reflection and consequence. It is built on a foundation of reason, but elevated by empathy. It understands that being good is not about obedience but intention, awareness, and responsibility.

That's the new moral compass: not north by doctrine, but by impact.

What reduces suffering? What promotes flourishing? What honors dignity, protects freedom, and builds a more just world — not for the saved or the chosen, but for everyone?

Religious morality may offer certainty. But certainty is not a virtue when it cannot be questioned. On the other hand, clarity is earned through reflection, self-correction, and the slow, deliberate work of becoming better than we were.

And so, morality without absolutes is not an empty frame. It's open— wide enough to hold complexity, contradiction, and growth. Wide enough to evolve with us.

In the next and final chapter, we will turn fully toward the unknown—not to conquer it or escape it, but to face it honestly. Once belief has been stripped away, once meaning is no longer inherited but made, we are left with the most important task of all: *to live without illusion and still find awe.*

7

The Freedom of Not Knowing

We have traced the arc of belief — from its evolutionary origins to its emotional utility, from its entanglement with identity to its resistance to evidence. We've challenged the comfort of certainty, dismantled the illusion of moral absolutes, and examined the possibility of a grounded, secular ethics. Along the way, a deeper question has emerged — quiet but persistent: *If we no longer know why we are here, can we still live as if it matters?*

This final chapter stands at that threshold.

Letting go of belief is not the end of a thought process. It's the beginning of something else. A kind of unarmed honesty. A life without a script. It's one thing to reject illusion; it's another to live without reaching for a new one. The terrain beyond dogma is unmarked. There are no signs pointing the way. No cosmic meaning. No promised reward. Only awareness — and the burden or possibility- comes with it.

This chapter is not about finding a substitute for faith. It's about learning to walk without it. It is about what remains when we stop needing certainty and start asking better questions—questions that don't pretend to close the gaps but that help us live inside them with clarity, humility, and intent.

Because the unknown is not something to escape, it's something to face. Not with answers, but with discipline. Not with submission, but with awe.

Certainty feels safe. It offers structure, continuity, and identity. It closes doors so that we don't have to. It spares us the weight of ambiguity by giving us final answers about life, death, morality, and meaning. This is what makes belief so enduring: not its evidence, but its efficiency. It relieves us of the need to search.

But that relief comes at a cost.

Certainty simplifies complexity. It flattens nuance into obedience. It replaces the evolving landscape of reality with a static picture that cannot be questioned without consequence. In this way, certainty isn't just a comfort. It's a defense system. It shields beliefs from revision, even when they cause harm. And the more emotionally tied we are to those beliefs, the more violently we protect them.

Earlier chapters explored how this rigidity manifests: how cognitive dissonance fuels denial, how identity fuses with belief, making any challenge feel like an attack on the self. Certainty, in this sense, is not just an intellectual stance—it's an emotional habit—one that resists interruption and growth.

Socrates was executed for asking too many questions, Galileo was silenced for describing the stars, and Darwin was ridiculed for suggesting we were not created but evolved. In each case, truth threatened certainty, and certainty struck back. The irony is that many of the comforts we now enjoy—modern medicine, human rights, freedom of thought—were born from doubt. They emerged not from those who clung to what they were told but from those willing to let go.

To abandon certainty is not to embrace chaos. It is to acknowledge reality: our understanding of the world is always partial and unfinished. That truth, if it exists, must be earned, not assumed.

There is a kind of grief that comes with this. A quiet sadness came from realizing that the frameworks that once explained everything no longer hold. This grief is often invisible. It doesn't get rituals. No one brings casseroles to the house of the newly secular. And yet, it is real. It lingers in the space where purpose used to be, where guidance once stood.

But it is not a dead end. It is a threshold.

In losing the borrowed answers, we are given permission to ask our own questions. In shedding the armor of identity, we begin to rebuild—not who we were told to be, but who we actually are. This grief is not a failure of strength. It is a sign of change. And like all transformation, it begins with letting go.

Certainty may feel warm. But clarity is what lets us breathe.

One of the most persistent myths is that meaning must be inherited, that without divine architecture, purpose disintegrates, and that without a higher plan, life becomes directionless. But this is a confusion between *given* meaning and *chosen* meaning, and the former has never been a guarantee of depth, only of certainty.

Metaphysical meaning—tied to fate, divine will, or cosmic design—offers emotional gravity. But it comes with strings. It often demands submission to an external story, a role written before we arrived. You are this. You were made for that. Your suffering serves a higher cause. In this narrative, meaning is not discovered through experience. It is imposed at birth. And once accepted, it resists revision.

But when the scaffolding falls — when gods disappear, when doctrines no longer persuade — the assumption is that meaning disappears with them. That which once felt sacred must now feel shallow.

This is not true.

Meaning they need not be inherited to be real. It can be made — consciously, deliberately, and without pretending to be eternal. We create meaning every time we choose to care. Not because someone commands it, but because we are capable of it. The fact that we can experience joy, grief, love, and awe — without an afterlife or being part of a divine plan — makes those experiences more fragile and valuable.

To raise a child, comfort a friend, create something beautiful, and reduce suffering — none of these require belief in a higher power. They only require presence. Intention. Attention. And a willingness to say: *This matters. Even if the universe doesn't notice, I do.*

This is meaning without metaphysics. Not an illusion, not a fantasy — but a conscious response to a world that owes us nothing. A world that will not tell us who we are, but will allow us to become it.

And in some ways, this is the more honest purpose — not because it lasts forever, but because it doesn't pretend to. It recognizes that life is short, meaning is provisional, and significance is something we grant rather than receive.

The absence of a cosmic plan doesn't strip life of meaning. It reveals that we are free to build it and are responsible for doing so.

There's a kind of awe that grows out of certainty—the awe of creation myths, divine purpose, and feeling watched and known by something greater. This awe doesn't come from what is observed but from what is believed. It's not about scale or detail—it's about story—the awe of being part of a plan.

But awe does not require answers. It never did.

Step outside on a cold night and look up. What you see isn't a ceiling or a dome. It's light from stars that died before your species began to write. It's energy stretched across time, touching the edge of your retina after traveling billions of years. It's not meant for you. It doesn't care that you're here. And somehow, that makes it even more magnificent.

This is what awe becomes without illusion. It is not the awe of being chosen. It is the awe of not being chosen, and still being conscious enough to know it.

Science does not offer comfort, but it provides perspective. And sometimes, perspective is enough. When Carl Sagan said, *"We are a way for the cosmos to know itself,"* he wasn't describing a metaphysical truth. He was articulating a fact: that out of all the entropy and decay, a cluster of carbon and electricity — the human brain — became able to reflect on its existence. That this has no inherent meaning doesn't make it meaningless. It makes it astonishing.

To look at a DNA strand, or a neuron, or a supernova — and to understand just *a fraction* of what it is — is a kind of reverence, not for what lies beyond explanation, but for what sits quietly within it. Wonder, stripped of superstition, does not shrink. It clarifies. It asks: *How is this even possible?* And then it listens, not for a voice from beyond the sky, but for an answer that may never come.

This kind of awe doesn't ask to be completed. It asks to be endured.

And that, too, is a kind of worship — not of gods, but of truth.

Without an afterlife, divine judgment, or cosmic justice, morality becomes more fragile and urgent. If this is the only life we get, then what we do with it matters in a way that eternity never could.

Immortality sedates responsibility. It suggests that justice will be served eventually, that pain will be redeemed, and that losses will be undone. But a finite existence offers no such reassurances. There is no reset, no celestial compensation. What is done is done. What is lost remains lost. And that starkness is what makes our choices real.

In a world without second chances beyond the grave, ethics become a present-tense obligation—not a ritual, not a rehearsal, but an immediate, unrepeatable act.

This is not a bleak conclusion. It is a demanding one.

It means that compassion is not something we can defer. It means that justice cannot be outsourced to a final reckoning. It means that the suffering of others, now, here, within this life, is our concern because no higher power is coming. Because we are it.

This urgency is not just moral. It's existential. The knowledge of death strips away abstraction. It exposes what's essential. It turns time into something precious — not because it leads to something greater, but because it ends. Meaning doesn't disappear in the face of death. It crystallizes.

We see this in how people behave when they are genuinely aware of mortality. They simplify, forgive, and reach out. They focus not on ideology or reputation but on connection, on presence, on what still can be said or done before the light goes out.

Religion tries to soften this finality. But in doing so, it also dilutes the intensity of life itself. When we imagine we'll get another chance, we don't hold this one as tightly. But when we know — deeply know — that this is it, we begin to live with sharper edges. And often, with greater care.

The end does not diminish the story. It gives it shape. A life that ends is not less meaningful. It is more focused. It is more deliberate. It invites us to act not because someone told us to or because someone is watching, but because *we choose to*. Because we are aware of the cost of inaction. Because we understand the weight of wasted time.

This is the morality of the finite, not less sacred than divine command, but more immediate. It demands nothing from eternity, only from us.

In a world without inherited certainty, one virtue becomes indispensable: humility. Not as self-deprecation, not as weakness, but as clarity, the recognition of our limits, and the discipline to live within them.

The deeper we dig into the nature of reality, the more we find ourselves confronted not with final answers, but with deeper questions. What caused the Big Bang? What lies beyond space and time? Why is there something rather than nothing? These are not puzzles to be solved by doctrine. They are edges of thought — places where certainty fractures and wonder begins.

Religious systems often offer closure in these moments. They supply answers when the questions become too large. But that closure comes at a price. It trades accuracy for comfort, humility for authority.

The scientific mind, by contrast, does not rush to fill the gap. It allows the unknown to remain unknown — not because it gives up, but because it refuses to pretend. It knows that honesty is more important than closure. That *"I don't know"* is not a failure of understanding, but a condition for growth.

This is intellectual humility. It is not an abdication of knowledge but a commitment to its process, a willingness to revise, to listen, and to remain open even when conviction feels easier. It is the posture that says, *"I could be wrong—and I want to know if I am."*

In earlier chapters, we explored how belief resists revision—how identity binds itself to ideas and defends them as if they were organs. Intellectual humility is the antidote to that rigidity. It does not ask for surrender. It asks for honesty. It doesn't weaken conviction—it refines it.

This humility also carries an ethical dimension. Being intellectually humble means recognizing that others may know what you do not. It opens the space for dialogue, for disagreement without contempt, for persuasion without coercion. It acknowledges that truth is not the property of any single person, group, or tradition — but something we approximate together, imperfectly.

In a culture built on performance and certainty, humility can feel like vulnerability. But it is not. It is resilience. It allows us to absorb new information without collapsing. It gives us the strength to say, "I was wrong," and the integrity to mean it.

The unknown is not a flaw in the system—it *is* the system. How we approach it—with arrogance or humility—determines what kind of thinkers we become.

We may never know why the universe exists or what preceded it. We may never find a final answer to the question of meaning. But we are not diminished by that lack of knowledge. We are defined by how we respond to it.

The most honest response is not silence, surrender, or a story. It is humility and the courage to keep walking forward anyway.

We began with a question—not just about what people believe but *why*—why belief persists, why it resists evidence, and why it so often survives in the face of contradiction. Along the way, we explored the architecture of the mind, the emotional power of certainty, the resistance to change, and the tools that allow us to think more clearly. We walked through the grief of leaving belief, the moral scaffolding that can stand without it, and the beauty that remains when illusions fall away.

And now we arrive here, not at a conclusion, but at a crossing.

The unknown is not something to be solved. It is something to live with. Something to face without flinching. Religion tried to erase it with story. Pseudoscience wanted to mask it with certainty. But the honest mind does neither. It acknowledges the unknown, not as failure, but as fact.

That's what it means to bridge the unknown. Not to conquer it. Not to escape it. But to stand at its edge and walk forward anyway.

There will be no revelations. No eternal answers. No voice from beyond the sky. But there will be something else—something harder, and more honest: a life lived without pretending.

In this space, morality becomes a choice, not a rule. Meaning becomes a project, not a plan. Truth becomes a discipline, not a possession. Awe becomes what it always was: the mind's response to reality when it stops demanding comfort and starts paying attention.

To live without illusion is not to be empty. It is to be free.

We do not need to know why we are here to act as if it matters that we are. In the absence of final answers, we are given something rarer — the freedom to choose better questions.

That freedom is not the end of wonder. It is its beginning.

Acknowledgments

This book was born from a question, and every page that followed was shaped by those willing to wrestle with the unknown. I am deeply grateful to the professors, authors, skeptics, and friends who challenged my thinking, not with certainty, but with better questions.

To the readers, mentors, and thinkers who offered their time, their minds, and their honesty: thank you. Your conversations, criticisms, and encouragement made this book sharper than I could have made it alone.

To those who walked away from certainty and kept going: this is for you.

References

Dawkins, Richard. *The God Delusion*. Houghton Mifflin, 2006.

Haidt, Jonathan. *The Righteous Mind: Why Good People Are Divided by Politics and Religion*. Pantheon Books, 2012.

Nietzsche, Friedrich. *The Gay Science*. Translated by Walter Kaufmann, Vintage Books, 1974.

Nietzsche, Friedrich. *Thus Spoke Zarathustra*. Translated by Walter Kaufmann, Penguin Classics, 1978.

Plato. *Euthyphro*. In *The Dialogues of Plato*, translated by Benjamin Jowett.

Popper, Karl. *Conjectures and Refutations: The Growth of Scientific Knowledge*. Routledge, 1963.

Sagan, Carl. *The Demon-Haunted World: Science as a Candle in the Dark*. Ballantine Books, 1995.

Darwin, Charles. *On the Origin of Species*. John Murray, 1859.

Galileo Galilei. *Dialogue Concerning the Two Chief World Systems*. Translated by Stillman Drake, University of California Press, 1953.

Socrates (via Plato). Referenced in multiple dialogues, particularly *Apology*, *Crito*, and *Euthyphro*.

If *Bridging the Unknown* sparked curiosity or challenged your perspective, the following works offer deeper insight, thoughtful challenge, and continued exploration:

Richard Dawkins – *The God Delusion*
A bold, evidence-based critique of religion and a defense of rational inquiry.

Carl Sagan – *The Demon-Haunted World: Science as a Candle in the Dark*
A timeless appeal for critical thinking and scientific literacy.

Jerry A. Coyne – *Why Evolution Is True*
An accessible, compelling explanation of the overwhelming evidence for evolution.

Steven Pinker – *Enlightenment Now*
A data-driven argument for science, reason, and human progress in the modern era.

Bertrand Russell – *Why I Am Not a Christian*
A classic philosophical essay dismantling religious arguments with clarity and wit.

Sam Harris – *The Moral Landscape*
Explores how science can guide moral values without invoking religion.